# DETENTE
## IN HISTORICAL PERSPECTIVE

The First CUNY Conference
on
History and Politics

**GEORGE SCHWAB, EDITOR**

**HENRY FRIEDLANDER, EDITOR**

**CYRCO PRESS    NEW YORK**

International Standard Book Number: 0-915326-01-9
Library of Congress Catalog Card Number: 75-5096
Cyrco Press, Inc., New York

# Contents

# PREFACE

On October 25 and 26, 1974, the first CUNY Conference on History and Politics was held at the Graduate Center of The City University of New York to examine the topic "Detente in Historical Perspective." This volume contains both the collected papers and an edited selection of the discussions which took place during that conference.

The political relations between the United States and the Soviet Union, the implications of former Chancellor Willy Brandt's *Ostpolitik*, and the continuing conflict in the Middle East have increased the urgency of the debate concerning detente. Obviously, we could not expect to resolve the fundamental problems surrounding detente. Rather, it was our more modest hope that such a conference might lead to formulating these problems in such a way that they might lend themselves to a more dispassionate and meaningful analysis. Perhaps the most difficult question was: *To what extent can genuine detente be brought about by two superpowers which have such radically divergent conceptions of the very nature of politics?*

Because the ongoing debate on detente has become somewhat repetitive we thought it timely to widen the scope of the discussion by focusing more precisely on the historical dimension. Hence, we set aside a considerable amount of time for an investigation of the period between the two world wars. Understandably, attention was focused on the years 1933–1939. In particular, it was hoped that the speakers would address themselves to the following question: *What do the words "appeasement" and "detente" connote in specific political situations, and what is the relationship between the two terms?*

Although history does not repeat itself, one may, nevertheless, attempt to draw broad parallels. Because Hitler had no border disputes with western states in 1939, it might be argued that appeasement or detente could have had a chance to work there. In the East, however, Hitler's territorial ambitions and ideological designs made war there seem almost inevitable, despite the Ribbentrop-Molotov Pact. Still, war between Germany on the one hand, and England and France on the other hand, opened that year because areas of conflict could not be isolated in Europe. Detente proved then to be indivisible.

In the same way, the Middle East has so far remained outside the area where detente appears to be working. Hence we must ask: *Can tensions between the United States and the Soviet Union be defused in one area —Europe—and not in another—the Middle East? In short, is detente divisible today?*

It would appear that the Soviet Union and the United States at the moment have no direct territorial designs in either Europe or the Middle East. Furthermore, because of the tensions between the Soviet Union and China it was in the Kremlin's interest to defuse political tensions with the West. To achieve this, Moscow had to soften her ideological posture vis-à-vis the Western world, something she proceeded to do. Nevertheless, the question still remains: *To what extent is her new ideological stand genuine, and to what extent is it merely a tactical response to a new challenge?*

The conference, in formal presentations and informal discussions, attempted to answer these and related questions. Panels of leading experts posed the questions and provided tentative answers. Discussion between the panelists and a specially invited distinguished audience raised further questions and provided additional viewpoints. In all, we believe the final product will appeal to a wide spectrum of readers, both laymen and specialists.

In organizing this conference acknowledgment is due to the Dean of Graduate Studies, Professor Hans J. Hillerbrand, for the financial and unswerving support he gave us. To his Executive Assistant, Mrs. Dorothy Weber, we are grateful for the many suggestions she has made, and for having helped us in a most gracious fashion with the numerous details that are involved in organizing a gathering of this sort.

We would also like to take this opportunity to express our appreciation to the President of the Graduate School, Harold M. Proshansky, for having in his welcoming remarks officially opened the First CUNY Conference on History and Politics.

To our friends and colleagues Professors Edward Rosen and Joel H. Wiener we acknowledge our gratitude for their encouragement of our endeavor, particularly when the burden of the conference appeared at moments to be insurmountable.

It would not be an overstatement to say that the form in which this volume appears is in large measure due to the skillful editorial advice we received from our friend and colleague, Frank D. Grande.

Also, we would like to take this opportunity to thank our editor at Cyrco Press, Ben Rosenzweig, for his patience and encouragement during the preparation of this volume. Naturally, we take the sole responsibility for anything that appears in this book.

GEORGE SCHWAB, Chairman
HENRY FRIEDLANDER, Co-chairman

# PART I
# HISTORICAL SETTING

# History and Politics:
# The Case of Detente

GERTRUDE HIMMELFARB

The subject of detente, both in its historical and contemporary sense, is so provocative that it may obscure the provocative nature of the series which this volume inaugurates. The theme of the series, "History and Politics," sounds innocent enough, but it is in fact a source of controversy in some circles. Academics are a contentious lot, prone to find matter for dispute where ordinary people would not. Certainly, few educated, well-informed laymen would find anything problematic in that conjunction of words, "History and Politics." They might see difficulties in the application of the theme to any particular circumstances—to the subject of detente, for example, in the inter-war years and the present. They might be troubled by the sometimes indiscriminate use of the words "detente" and "appeasement" in these periods. They might quarrel over terminology, shifts in usage, the analogies and metaphors by which the past is made to inform the present and the present the past. All of these are obviously open to dispute.

What is less obvious, but what has given concern to some

historians and philosophers, is whether history and politics can *ever* be joined together without doing violence to both, without violating the uniqueness, the particularity, of any event in the past and any situation in the present. The historian Herbert Butterfield has warned us against imposing our consciousness of the present upon the past, against reading history backwards, projecting upon the past our hindsight knowledge of what was to come, trying to use the past to illuminate, even solve, the problems of the present. He has described this tendency as "the Whig interpretation of history," or, as it is familiarly known to graduate students, "the Whig fallacy."

The philosopher Michael Oakeshott has made the same point in somewhat different terms. On the question of the utility of history—whether there are any practical lessons to be derived from the past, whether history can ever intelligently, legitimately, inform politics—Oakeshott is uncompromising and unequivocal. History, he insists, has no practical utility; there are no political lessons to be learned from it. The only proper attitude for the historian is that of contemplation and enjoyment. He can only contemplate the past *in* itself and enjoy it *for* itself. Knowing Oakeshott, we can be certain that he does not intend this as a denigration of history. On the contrary, for him contemplation and enjoyment are of the highest philosophical and human value. He expressed this belief in his inimitable manner in a passage that few philosophers or historians—probably no *male* philosopher or historian—would venture to quote today.

> The 'historian' adores the past; but the world today has perhaps less place for those who love the past than ever before. . . It wishes only to learn from the past and it constructs a 'living past' which repeats with spurious authority the utterances put into its mouth. But to the 'historian' this is a piece of obscene necromancy: the past he adores is dead. The world has neither love nor respect for what is dead, wishing only to recall it to life again. It deals with the past as with a man, expecting it to talk sense and have something to say ap-

posite to its plebeian 'causes' and engagements. For the 'historian,' for whom the past is dead and irreproachable, the past is feminine. He loves it as a mistress of whom he never tires and whom he never expects to talk sense.[1]

Oakeshott notwithstanding, most of us do expect history to "talk sense." For all of our wariness of historical analogies we cannot help looking for meaning in history. What Butterfield and Oakeshott have properly alerted us to is the need to see the past undistorted by our view of the present, to understand the past in its own terms and for its own sake. But this does not mean that the past is of no use to the present. It does mean that its utility derives not from the identity of words—"detente" or "appeasement"—nor from the similarity of events—agreements followed by aggression—but from the meaning of those words and events: the limits of national interest and international cooperation, the relationship of ideology and policy, the nature of *Realpolitik* and statecraft. The lessons of history, in short, are conveyed to us by way of principles rather than analogies. It is thus that the past informs the present. And it is in this sense that the theme, "History and Politics," becomes of crucial significance.

[1]Michael Oakeshott, "The Activity of Being An Historian," *Rationalism in Politics* (New York: Basic Books, 1962), p. 166.

# DETENTE 1919-1939:
# A STUDY IN FAILURE

KEITH EUBANK

On September 30, 1938, at Heston airport, when Neville Chamberlain stepped from the airplane that had brought him back from Munich, he waved a paper to the crowd and cried: "I've got it! I've got it!"

To the happy throng he exclaimed: "This morning I had another talk with the German Chancellor, Herr Hitler, and here is the paper which bears his name upon it as well as mine." The delighted but exhausted prime minister proceeded to read the contents to his audience.

That document, drafted by Chamberlain and signed by him and by Hitler, was another chapter in the search for detente. The search had continued for two decades; it would end only in another and more horrible conflict. Perhaps there is some value to be gained from an examination of the efforts made in those two decades to achieve a detente.

To avoid war, nations have sought policies which would relax international tensions and at the same time defuse situations that could lead to armed conflict. Since the French for so long influenced the language of modern diplomacy, the word "detente" has been used to designate such a policy. It means a "reduction of tension between states, an improvement of international relations." It comes from the verb, "detendre," meaning "to relax, to unbend a bow, to evolve toward appeasement."

Most recently the word and the policy which it denotes have become almost daily reading in American newspapers, thanks to the negotiating efforts of Henry Kissinger in his dealings with the Soviet Union and the Peoples' Republic of

China. The policy had an interesting history before Mr. Kissinger converted it into a sorely needed virtue for the administration of Richard Nixon.

In the years 1919-1939, the policy of detente was most conspicuous as applied to Germany by various British governments. The French, for reasons of national security as well as history, were never as ardent as the British in seeking a policy of detente. They accepted detente but with great reluctance. In considering detente, our concern will be with the policies pursued by British governments in their labors to tidy up the problems left over from the great war of 1914-1918.

The end of the war left the victorious powers with the problem of Germany—what to do with an industrialized, well educated, vigorous nation that was right in the center of Europe, where it could cause the most trouble. Its might had been proven in the bloody battles of the war—the Marne, Tannenberg, Verdun, Jutland, Passchendaele. When peace came on November 11, 1918, it was necessary to decide on the future of Germany.

The French had their answer: occupy, divide, and detach. But the French solution was set aside for that preferred by Woodrow Wilson and David Lloyd George. Only part of Germany would be occupied; some sections would be annexed by Germany's neighbors; and areas such as the Rhineland would not be permanently detached. Nevertheless, the Treaty of Versailles resulted in a Germany that felt abused, raped, and betrayed. The Germans resented the loss of territory and the forced reduction in their military forces, as well as the obligation to pay reparations. The German people believed that the Treaty of Versailles was unfair and that it should be revised. It was in this situation that the search for detente began.

The yearning for detente stemmed from a strong feeling, peculiar to the British, that the Treaty of Versailles was unfair and had somehow to be revised and that the war between Britain and Germany had been a terrible mistake. It must not happen again. To avoid such a catastrophe, international tensions must be relaxed and defused. Britain would take on the responsibility of working for a detente, and if need be, acting as the mediator between France and Germany.

The seekers for detente originally believed that if there could be a comprehensive, general settlement of the problems troubling the Germans, a settlement agreed to by the Germans and approved by the French, then a detente would be achieved which would usher in an era of confidence and peace. Moreover, Europe would be so pleased with the new condition and its effects that the economy would soar to new heights. If there were peace then Britain could cut back on armaments and lower taxes. The seekers after detente believed that another dictated treaty must be avoided at all costs, for that would only rile the Germans. A freely negotiated settlement was the answer, an agreement that would be upheld and observed by the German government and the people.

In this process British diplomats and politicians often associated detente with a word that was to be damned in the late 1930's—appeasement. Actually the word, "appeasement," was used throughout the inter-war period in a perfectly respectable manner. Often both "detente" and "appeasement" were used interchangeably by British spokesmen. "Appeasement," however, did not mean to surrender to the bully's demand, but rather to "pacify, to quiet, to soothe." It would seem then that in order to achieve appeasement, one party could resort to a policy of detente. From the evidence of the two decades there was a very strong connection between detente and appeasement. But it must be understood that in resorting to appeasement it was never intended to have nations surrender their vital interests in order to avoid war. That has become the popular meaning of "appeasement," not the meaning of those who sought detente.

The British took up the task of achieving a detente when

the United States Senate refused to ratify the Treaty of
Versailles and the French set out to enforce the Treaty to
the letter. To many in London, it all looked like a French
plot to play Napoleon again. They feared that the French,
in their hatred, were laying the groundwork for another
war, just as the Treaty of Frankfurt had helped ignite the
war in 1914. To avoid this mistake, the British wanted the
Treaty of Versailles revised and Germany appeased. After
all, John Maynard Keynes had pointed the way in his book,
*The Economic Consequences of the Peace.* There had to be
a general agreement which would resolve all of the troubles
left over from the war. For these were like an unresolved
chord hanging on the ear that clamored to be resolved. But
resolution proved difficult.

The first effort at detente resulted from a split between
Britain and France over the question of reparations, with
London more concerned with restoring German credits and
Paris more inclined to make the defeated pay through the
nose. After Germany was declared in default in her reparations payments, French and Belgian troops occupied the
Ruhr in 1923 to insure payment by collecting them on the
spot. London was infuriated; all this increased tension and
impeded detente. Soon the French found that occupation
was not the cure-all for the reparations problem, and that
the German government, led by Gustav Stresemann, was
all too aware of the price that was being paid for
resistance—inflation and disunity. Finally, to the delight of
the British, both sides agreed to accept the Dawes Plan
drafted by a committee of experts.

In the summer of 1924, the acceptance of the Dawes
Plan was solemnized at the London Conference. By then J.
Ramsay MacDonald, a pacifist, had become prime minister
as well as foreign secretary; he was eager to be rid of the
Treaty of Versailles in order to reach a detente with Germany. He was happy to preside over the London Conference where it was agreed that the French would evacuate
the Ruhr, and that Germany would accept reparations at a

reduced rate. To soften any German bitterness over accepting the Dawes Plan, American loans would be made to Germany, but not to France or to Britain. It was a happy hour for MacDonald because he believed that a detente had been achieved. He informed the delegates:

> We are now offering the first really negotiated agreement since the war; every party here represented is morally bound to do its best to carry it out because it is not the result of an ultimatum; we have tried to meet each other as far as the public opinion of the various countries would allow us. This agreement may be regarded as the first peace treaty, because we sign it with a feeling that we have turned our backs on the terrible years of war and war mentality.[1]

But the hoped-for detente had not yet arrived. In December 1924, unhappy with the Germans because they had not fully complied with the disarmament provisions of the Treaty of Versailles, the Western Powers—France, Britain, Belgium, and Italy—informed Berlin that the scheduled evacuation of Cologne in January 1925 would not take place. This crisis, plus the rumor that Britain and France were about to conclude a military alliance, led Stresemann to propose the Rhineland Pact which involved German acceptance of the status quo in Western Europe and an international guarantee of the demilitarized Rhineland. Stresemann's proposal ended up in the Locarno Treaty, initialed in October 1925 by representatives of Britain, France, Germany, Belgium, and Italy.

Was this not at last the hoped-for detente? Through its provisions, Britain could deter Germany and pacify the French, without being forced to take sides. At the same time Europe would not be divided into competing alliance systems. Above all, Germany accepted the Locarno Treaty voluntarily as an equal to the other signatory powers.

Austen Chamberlain, the British Foreign Secretary, informed the House of Commons, "We regard Locarno, not as the end of the work of appeasement and reconciliation, but as its beginning."

A Foreign Office official commented on the results of Locarno:

> A detente has certainly been achieved. . . . No longer is western Europe divided into two camps—the victors and vanquished. At Locarno the ex-enemies met on a footing of perfect equality. . . . The work done by the Dawes scheme has been consolidated. The remaining problems which threatened to throw Europe back into chaos have either been solved or are on the way to solution. . . . Locarno is but a first step. It is an omen of an international spirit which, if fostered, will lead to far more than practical men have ever dared to hope since the war.[2]

But British delight over Locarno and the resulting detente soon changed. For they discovered that instead of the Germans being pacified because of the detente, they only made more demands for concessions from the western powers before signing the Locarno agreements in December 1925.[3]

In February 1926, Chamberlain complained to Lord D'Abernon, the British ambassador in Germany:

> What has been Germany's reply [to the Allied evacuation of Cologne and to concessions on disarmament]? In hardly a single point have the German government come forward with any offer to meet our desires. . . . Nor is that all: for not only have the German government taken no practical steps to meet us, but they have so far as is apparent made no attempt to check the vituperative abuse with which German statesmen and the German press have greeted our every endeavour to act up to the Locarno spirit. The only reply to each measure of conciliation on our part is an angry complaint that more has not been granted. . . . British policy is unchanged, but

Locarno implied mutual concessions. It requires reciprocity from Germany for its development and cannot be worked by one side only; nor can it be developed by means of threats. The Germans must show the goodwill which they expect us to show them; but in their debates and resolutions no sign is to be found of the Locarno spirit, nothing but ever growing demands put forward almost as ultimatums.[4]

Chamberlain's angry outburst touched on the key to any successful detente: reciprocity. For detente to succeed, it had to work both ways. All parties had to understand what it meant to the others who were involved. Here was the root of the problem of detente in the 1920's: it meant different things to the British and to the Germans.

London thought of detente in terms of improving business and helping the British economy. It would also prevent any need to rearm, which involved the raising of taxes. But to the Germans it was one means of ultimately revising the Treaty of Versailles and finally doing away with it. When that occurred, Germany wanted to be back in the position of power formerly enjoyed before the outbreak of war in 1914, plus some additional advantages.

Detente surfaced again when the Hague Conference met in August 1929 to consider the report of the committee which had produced the Young Plan. The conference became the stage for a confrontation between the former allies over the future of Germany. The British delegation, led by Philip Snowden, chancellor of the Exchequer, beat down the French and compelled them to agree to the evacuation of the Rhineland ahead of the schedule laid down in the Treaty of Versailles. All troops would be withdrawn by June 30, 1930, five years ahead of schedule, the reparation payments owed by Germany were reduced by approximately 20 percent, and a limit was placed on the schedule of payments. The results of the Hague Conference seemed to those who sought a detente "to offer hope that international tensions, especially the longstanding Franco-German feud, might be finally dying away.[5]

It was the hope of the British government, once more led

by MacDonald, that Germany would become more content and satisfied. At that time, the policy of conciliation was regarded as enlightened, a major step in the achievement of detente. But as before, once more there were demands from Germany for concessions. Now it was the Saar. And when the Allied troops left the Rhineland in 1930, no gratitude was expressed by the German government. There were even hints that the demilitarization should be ended. Although the British were exasperated, they did not give up hope of reaching a detente.

They tried again in the Lausanne Conference in 1932 where reparations were in effect ended. The British hoped that the conference would lead to more far-reaching agreements which would make peace long lasting. Neville Chamberlain, chancellor of the Exchequer, concluding for the British delegation, declared: "From the first, we have all been sustained by the thought that the future happiness of millions of human beings might depend upon the results that we could achieve here. . . . The British Delegation is proud to have taken part in a work which we believe will prove the beginning of happier times for us all."[6] But it was not to be.

In February 1932, when the Disarmament Conference at last convened in Geneva, the stage was set for another try at detente by the British. Time, however, was running out because Adolf Hitler and his Nazi Party daily grew stronger as the depression undermined the Weimar republic. During the Disarmament Conference, Britain pressed France to surrender military superiority to satisfy the German clamor for equality in armaments. If such a compromise could be attained, it would break the disarmament deadlock and open the way to detente. Before that goal could be achieved, Hitler came to power in January 1933. Shortly afterward, in a conference with his generals, he declared: "Rebuilding of the armed forces is the most important prerequisite for attaining the goal: reconquest of political power. Universal military service has to come back."[7]

When the German delegation left the Disarmament Conference in October 1933, acting under Hitler's orders, it was a setback for the cause of detente. Nevertheless, the British government, headed by MacDonald, did not give up the quest for detente. To this end, MacDonald personally suggested that Hitler visit London. The official German reply to the idea of inviting Hitler to London was "absurd."[8]

For the next eighteen months, MacDonald and his ministers worked on a disarmament agreement with Germany as a prologue to detente. Early in January 1934, the Mac Donald government informed Hitler that "a general agreement securing the limitation of armaments at the lowest practicable level would be the most effective and significant proof of international appeasement and an encouragement of the mutual confidence which springs from good and neighborly relations. Consequently, His Majesty's Government regard agreement about armaments not as an end in itself, but rather as a concomitant of world peace and as an outcome of political amelioration."[9]

To explain this proposal and to learn Hitler's reactions, young Anthony Eden was dispatched to Berlin in February 1934. There Hitler explained that he would not consider the Treaty of Versailles binding on Germany; he would only observe those treaties freely entered into by Germany. According to Hitler, Germany wanted only defensive weapons; if other nations would join in an agreement, she would renounce military aviation as well.

Hitler seemed sympathetic to the cause of detente. "For 14 years," he said, "he had advocated the idea of understanding between Germany and England, although he had met with vigorous resistance on this matter within Germany. . . . He was of the opinion that owing to their spiritual and racial kinship the two nations were predestined for harmonious cooperation in sincere friendship."[10]

These sentiments were contradicted by the report that Germany had beefed up the military budget for 1934-35. This became the excuse for the French to reject legalizing

German rearmament. Already the French military intelligence services had reported that by 1938 Germany would possess an army superior to the French army, and "far more powerful than the German army of 1914."[11]

Although this report was passed on to London, the Mac Donald government, ignoring it, worked to bury Part V of the Treaty of Versailles, relating to disarmament. The corpse would be interred through an agreement legalizing German rearmament, which was well under way. The burial would save everybody's face. In addition, it was hoped that detente would be aided by "a general settlement reached by free negotiation between Germany and the other powers. . . . It would also be part of the general settlement that Germany would resume her place in the League of Nations with a view to active membership."[12]

But in March 1935, Hitler killed Part V when he announced German rearmament publicly. Nevertheless, still eager for detente, Sir John Simon, the foreign secretary, and Eden went to Berlin and talked with Hitler in March 1935. From their discussions emerged nothing but the decision to negotiate an Anglo-German Naval agreement. This pact, signed in June 1935, seemed to its supporters in Britain as a giant step toward detente. To them it signified an end to the naval rivalry which had poisoned the pre-1914 years. Most important, it was an attempt to take Hitler at his word when he insisted that he would observe an agreement freely negotiated by Germany.

The search for detente continued, even though Hitler violated the Locarno Agreement when he ordered his troops into the Rhineland on March 7, 1936. The outbreak of the Spanish Civil War in July 1936 made detente more urgent. British foreign policy, however, tended to drift, thanks to Stanley Baldwin, who had succeeded MacDonald as prime minister. In May 1937 Baldwin retired in favor of Neville Chamberlain, the chancellor of the Exchequer, who wanted an end to the drifting foreign policy. Chamberlain was a seasoned, tough politician who could be ruthless when necessary. A shy, reserved man, he liked order, abhorred war, and looked for solutions to problems.

On the eve of Baldwin's retirement, Chamberlain had expounded his views on foreign policy in a memorandum to the Cabinet Committee on Foreign Policy.

> It will, I think, be admitted that the general situation in Europe is such that we cannot afford to miss any opportunity of reducing the international tension. . . . Even a slight improvement in the international atmosphere may lead gradually to general detente, whereas a policy of drift may lead gradually to general war. . . . Our objective should be to set out the political guarantees which we want from Germany as part of any general settlement. . . .[13]

The program which Chamberlain wanted to propose to Germany included a security pact for western Europe to replace the Locarno Treaty, Hitler's assurance that he would respect the independence and territorial integrity of the nations in central Europe, the return of Germany to the League of Nations, and of course an arms limitation agreement.

No progress was made toward detente during the summer of 1937. In the fall, Lord Halifax, lord president of the council, received an invitation from Hermann Göring to attend the International Sporting Exhibition in Berlin. At the insistence of the German government, a request was made for a meeting with Hitler. Chamberlain, eager for personal contact with Hitler, accepted the invitation and packed Halifax off to Berlin and from there to Berchtesgaden.

At their meeting, Halifax outlined the basis for detente:

> There were no doubt other questions arising out of the Versailles settlement which seemed to us capable of causing trouble if they were unwisely handled, e.g., Danzig, Austria, Czechoslovakia. On all these matters we were not necessarily concerned to stand up for the status quo as to-day, but we were concerned to avoid such treatment of them as would be

likely to cause trouble. If reasonable settlements could be reached with the free assent and goodwill of those primarily concerned, we certainly had no desire to block [them].[14]

This news must have delighted Hitler, who declared that only one question stood between Germany and Britain: colonies.

Back in London, Halifax reported to Chamberlain on the results of his meeting with Hitler. "The German visit," wrote Chamberlain, "was from my point of view a great success, because it achieved its object, that of creating an atmosphere in which it is possible to discuss with Germany the practical questions involved in a European settlement. . . . I don't see why we shouldn't say to Germany, 'give us satisfactory assurances that you won't use force to deal with the Austrians and Czechoslovakians, and we will give you similar assurances that we won't use force to prevent the changes you want if you can get them by peaceful means.' "[15] The prospects for detente seemed on the rise.

Chamberlain decided that Britain must take the first step toward detente by putting forward concrete proposals. It was with this aim in mind that the British ambassador, Nevile Henderson, presented Chamberlain's program for detente to Hitler on March 3, 1938. It was aimed at establishing "the basis for a genuine and cordial friendship with Germany, beginning with an improvement of the atmosphere and ending with the creation of a new spirit of friendly understanding." Britain wanted to collaborate in a settlement "based on reason." The deal offered Hitler included colonies for Germany in Africa, arms limitation, and a German contribution to the peace and security of central Europe. The meeting was a total disaster. Hitler denounced the British press as the greatest threat to international security. As for central Europe, "Germany," ranted Hitler, "would not tolerate interference by third powers in the settlement of her relations with kindred countries or with countries having large German elements in their population." A scowling Führer warned: "Once Germans were fired upon in Austria or Czechoslovakia, the German Reich would intervene."[16]

Neither Henderson's report of the meeting with Hitler nor the *Anschluss* on March 12, 1938, altered Chamberlain's campaign for detente. It only changed direction, focusing on Czechoslovakia and the Sudeten German minority problem. In meetings with the Cabinet Committee on Foreign Policy in March 1938, Chamberlain laid down the policy that would be followed in the next few months and that would culminate in the Munich Conference. No guarantee would be given to Czechoslovakia, but instead some arrangement for Sudeten autonomy would be developed. Through this method it was hoped that the situation in Czechoslovakia would be defused and the tension relaxed.

By the end of April, Chamberlain and Halifax, now the foreign secretary, had compelled Edouard Daladier, the French premier, and Georges Bonnet, the foreign minister, to join in pressuring the Czechoslovak government into negotiating with the Sudeten German representatives. The Czechs were instructed to work quickly with the aim of reaching a "comprehensive and lasting settlement." At the same time, Berlin was asked to influence the Sudeten Germans to moderate their demands. If cooperation could be secured from everyone, then they would be on the way to achieving detente. Chamberlain's dream of detente was suddenly wrecked by the May Crisis, when rumors of German troop movements along the Czechoslovak frontier led to the mobilization of Czech troops. As a result, the negotiations bogged down and Chamberlain's hopes for an immediate detente dissipated.

Because his grand design for pacifying Germany and achieving detente seemed in danger, Chamberlain dispatched a "mediator," Walter Runciman, a millionaire experienced in banking and shipping, to Prague to tighten the screws. Under pressure from both London and Paris, the

Czechs made concessions to the Sudeten Germans. Meanwhile, reports that Germany was mobilizing for war multiplied. Suddenly, the Czech-Sudeten negotiations collapsed following Sudeten Nazi rioting in the Sudetenland. In Paris there was panic; Chamberlain had to do something to stop the war. For sometime, Chamberlain had been considering that he ought to take a more personal role in working for the detente. He decided to fly to Germany and there to propose to Hitler personally that a plebiscite be used to solve the Sudeten minority questions and that a multinational guarantee be given for the remainder of Czechoslovakia. "The inducement to be held out to Herr Hitler in the proposed negotiations," he informed the Cabinet, "was the chance of securing better relations between Germany and England."[17] To this end, Chamberlain asked for and received an invitation from Hitler to meet with him at Berchtesgaden.

There in his private meeting with Hitler on September 15, Chamberlain tried to be firm but the Führer, after putting on his act about the poor suffering Sudeten Germans, threatened war. His price for keeping the peace was the cession of the Sudetenland to Germany. Chamberlain avoided bargaining, accepted Hitler's proposal, and returned home. There he told the Cabinet: "The impression left on me was that Herr Hitler meant what he said. . . . My view is that Herr Hitler was telling the truth."[18]

The rest of the story is well known: the Czech government forced to agree to cede strategic territory, Chamberlain's return to Germany, and new demands made by Hitler at Godesberg. At this point, instead of walking out of the negotiations, Chamberlain stayed. He did not want to ruin any opportunity for detente, but Chamberlain had undermined his own bargaining position. He had done worse than that because in his panic he had permitted the search for detente to degenerate into a surrender to threats.

Back in London, Chamberlain asked the Cabinet to accept the Godesberg demands. He based his request on the assertion that Hitler had promised to make no more territorial demands and had vowed that if the Sudeten question "can be settled peacefully, it might be a turning point in Anglo-German relations." In his eagerness to convince the Cabinet, Chamberlain declared: "It would be a great tragedy if we lost this opportunity. A peaceful settlement of Europe depended upon an Anglo-German understanding. . . . I have now established an influence over Hitler, and he trusts me and is willing to work with me."[19]

At that point, Chamberlain was thwarted by a split in the Cabinet. The French got their backs up, and the Czechs rejected the Godesberg demands. War seemed a matter of days, if not hours, after Chamberlain reluctantly agreed that his government would back the French if they went to the aid of Czechoslovakia.

Then Bonnet and Chamberlain, each independently of the other, proposed to Hitler that they compel Czech acceptance of whatever he wished. By offering Hitler a blank check, they had changed negotiation into capitulation. Chamberlain offered to make another trip to Germany if it would please Hitler. Even Benito Mussolini was involved in the negotiations out of which came the invitation to the notorious Munich Conference. There the four leaders —Chamberlain, Hitler, Daladier, and Mussolini—carved up Czechoslovakia in the name of peace. At the end of the conference, Chamberlain and Hitler signed a private agreement. It was Chamberlain's prescription for detente.

> We regard the agreement signed last night and the Anglo-German Naval Agreement as symbolic of the desire of our two peoples never to go to war with one another again. We are resolved that the method of consultation shall be the method adopted to deal with any other questions that may concern our two countries, and we are determined to continue our efforts to remove possible sources of difference and thus to contribute to assure the peace of Europe.[20]

To the end of his life, Neville Chamberlain never regretted what he had done at Munich. But he had deceived himself with the delusion that his private agreement with Hitler was truly the opening of a detente. On March 15, 1939, when German troops occupied Bohemia and Moravia, Chamberlain learned how much Hitler valued the Munich Agreement and that private agreement which he had waved at the Heston airport.

Yet even after these disappointments, Chamberlain hoped for a detente. When it became necessary to issue a warning to Hitler about Poland, on March 31, 1939, Chamberlain still hoped that the warning would bring Hitler to his senses, and lead him ultimately to a detente. Chamberlain never expected that it would ultimately result in a world war.[21]

In the summer of 1939, after Czechoslovakia had lost its independence and Poland's security was imperiled, Chamberlain made a secret offer to Hitler which included a pact renouncing the use of force, a promise of non-interference in each other's sphere of influence, a revision of the sections of the Treaty of Versailles relating to colonies, an arms limitation agreement, more extensive economic arrangements, and a loan of £500,000,000 to Germany.[22] Britain would forget about the public pledge made by Chamberlain to help Poland, and Hitler could have Danzig. Thus did detente turn into farce. Hitler never took up the offer which became the final effort to reach that elusive detente before the outbreak of war.

In the two decades between the wars, the desire for detente was a direct outgrowth of the widespread aversion in Britain to another conflict similar to that of 1914-1918, which many were convinced, thanks to the work of revisionist historians, was the result of an accident which could have been avoided. Many believed that France and Russia were more responsible for the war than was Germany. Detente was also a product of the embarrassment over the punitive clauses in the Treaty of Versailles which, it was thought, should be revised.

For detente to have been successful, agreement was

necessary about its meaning and its use. In the 1920's, the British aimed at detente through a revision of the Treaty of Versailles. Those favorable to revision of the Treaty imagined that a people as rational as the Germans would welcome revision and participate wholeheartedly in a detente. But the German government saw detente as a device, not to revise, but to revoke the Treaty of Versailles. Revocation was never the intention of the British because it would have meant restoring Germany to the position of power which she had before November 11, 1918. In the 1920's that was a dose the French would not swallow.

When Hitler came to power, the prospects for detente worsened because he wanted not only to revoke the Treaty of Versailles but to put Germany in a position to dominate Europe, even at the risk of war. To Hitler, detente, so dear to those silly Englishmen, was only a means to an end: aggression.

Those Englishmen who made up the British establishment, Victorian in upbringing and evangelical in religion, could not comprehend Hitler's intentions. No sane person would consciously wish to go to war again. They reasoned that Hitler was the leader of the German people, leaders must be rational people, detente is a rational policy, therefore, the German leaders will welcome detente, for it is a policy of appeasement. If Hitler made some wild statements in public, he was only showing his deep concern for the German minorities. His statements were purely political rhetoric, intended for home consumption. He would never deliberately choose war. After all, wars come about because of bizarre incidents such as the assassination of the Archduke Franz Ferdinand. This line of reasoning made detente sensible to the British. However, because of the wide gulf between Hitler's intentions and the outlook of the British, detente was doomed to fail.

Detente, like other policies, once set in operation, takes on a life of its own, defying efforts to change it even when the available information underlines the need either to rethink the policy, curtail it, or kill it. Moreover, no politician wishes to admit that his policy has failed, particularly when it has widespread popular support as detente did in Britain. There successive governments refused to reverse the policy even when a flood of reports revealed that detente was not succeeding. Advocates of detente preferred to ignore negative information and to continue the policy. They were finally caught in a trap.

They had to accede to the demands of the opposing party in order to avoid rupturing the detente. Consequently they avoided bargaining, accepted Hitler's demands in order to preserve the semblance of detente. Even if Czechoslovakia had to be torn apart, Chamberlain consented to "self-determination" for the Sudeten Germans for the sake of the anticipated detente. Actually, by September 15 he was really more concerned with avoiding a war, for which Britain was unprepared, than with a detente. By acceding to Hitler's demands, Chamberlain let detente degenerate into surrender in the face of threats—a condition that has become known now as "appeasement."

For detente to succeed it must not be blatantly exploited for the benefit of one party at the expense of the other as it was in the 1920's and the 1930's. Its success requires reciprocity, sincerity, and agreement on the basic issues. These conditions were present in the detente between Britain and France, concluded in the Entente Cordiale on April 8, 1904. In that agreement both parties buried their quarrels and ended decades of bickering over colonies. The Entente Cordiale was a successful detente because Britain and France had much in common, including fear. Both feared being dragged into the Russo-Japanese War; they also feared the German Empire. In the 1930's there was a difference: Britain feared war, Hitler welcomed it.

Detente also became a personal matter, then and now. Recently we have been told that a president and the secretary of state had to be retained in office because they alone could manage detente. Their personal contact with opposing national leaders was indispensable; without it detente would fail. Neville Chamberlain also tied his reputation to detente. In his conceit he imagined that he had attained an influence over Hitler, who trusted the British politician so much that he was willing to make a private agreement with him. It was this personal involvement which led Chamberlain foolishly to persist in detente long after it should have been ended.

Unfortunately, Hitler did not reciprocate in his regard for Chamberlain. After the Munich Conference he told his entourage: "If ever that silly old man comes interfering here again with his umbrella, I'll kick him downstairs and jump on his stomach in front of photographers."[23]

In the future, perhaps, advocates of detente ought to have on their desks as a reminder of the pitfalls of detente, a large, glossy picture of Neville Chamberlain at Heston airport waving that piece of paper. He too believed that he had achieved a detente.

## NOTES

1. Arnold J. Toynbee, *Survey of International Affairs, 1924* (London: Oxford University Press, 1928), p. 384.

2. Martin Gilbert, *The Roots of Appeasement* (London: Weidenfeld and Nicolson, 1966), p. 115; "Foreign Office Memorandum Respecting the Locarno Treaties," January 10, 1926, *Documents on British Foreign Policy* (cited hereafter as *DBFP*) Series 1A, Volume 1 (London: Her Majesty's Stationery Office, 1966), p. 16.

3. Austen Chamberlain to Lord D'Abernon, November 4, 1925, *ibid.*, pp. 88–89; Chamberlain to Lord Crewe and Lord D'Abernon, November 8, 1925, *ibid.*, pp. 111-112.

4. Chamberlain to Lord D'Abernon, February 1, 1926, *ibid.*, p. 381.

5. David Carlton, *MacDonald versus Henderson. The Foreign Policy of the Second Labour Government* (London: Macmillan, 1970), p. 57.

6. July 8, 1932, *DBFP*, Series 2, Volume 3, p. 427.

7. February 3, 1933, *Documents on German Foreign Policy*

*1918–1945* (cited hereafter as *DGFP*) Series C, Volume 1 (Washington: United States Government Printing Office, 1957), p. 37.

8. Neurath to Hoesch, November 11, 1933, *ibid.*, Volume 2, p. 106.

9. Foreign Office memorandum, January 25, 1934, *DBFP*, Series 2, Volume 6, pp. 314-324.

10. Memorandum of a conversation, Hitler-Eden, February 20, 1934, *DGFP*, Series C, Volume 2, pp. 513-518.

11. Tyrell to Simon, December 6, 1933, *DBFP*, Series 2, Volume 6, p. 164.

12. Anglo-French memorandum, February 3, 1935, *ibid.*, Volume 12, pp. 482-484.

13. As quoted in Ian Colvin, *The Chamberlain Cabinet* (New York: Taplinger Publishing Company, 1971), pp. 39-40.

14. As quoted in Correlli Barnett, *The Collapse of British Power* (New York: William Morrow and Company, 1972), p. 467.

15. As quoted in Keith Feiling, *The Life of Neville Chamberlain* (London: Macmillan and Company, 1946), pp. 332-333.

16. Ribbentrop to Henderson, March 4, 1938, *DGFP*, Series D, Volume 1, pp. 240-249.

17. As quoted in Keith Middlemas, *Diplomacy of Illusion: The British Government and Germany, 1937-39* (London: Weidenfeld and Nicolson, 1972), pp. 334–335.

18. As quoted in Roger Parkinson, *Peace for our Time* (New York: David McKay Company, 1972), p. 28.

19. *Ibid.*, p. 41.

20. Notes of Conversation between Chamberlain and Hitler, September 30, 1938, *DBFP*, Series 3, Volume 2, pp. 635-640.

21. *Cf.* Keith Eubank, "The British Pledge to Poland: Prelude to War," *Southwestern Social Science Quarterly*, Vol. XLV, March, 1965, 340-348.

22. Martin Gilbert and Martin Gott, *The Appeasers* (Boston: Houghton Mifflin, 1963), pp. 219–225; Leonard Mosley, *On Borrowed Time* (New York: Random House, 1969), pp. 261-265; Wohltat's report on his talk with Horace Wilson, July 24, 1939, *DGFP*, Series D, Volume VI, pp. 978-981.

23. Ivone Kirkpatrick, *The Inner Circle* (London: Macmillan and Company, 1959), p. 135.

# Detente and Appeasement from a Political Scientist's Vantage-Point

## John H. Herz

Professor Eubank has presented vividly the sad and sordid story of how sincere and well-intentioned efforts to arrive at detente in the Europe of the interwar period turned into "appeasement" in the pejorative sense this term had acquired at and through Munich. In our days the term detente seems to undergo a transformation in meaning similar to that which appeasement underwent in the earlier period, namely, from a genuine effort to arrive at mutual understanding to a policy of unilateral concessions. At the end of his paper, Mr. Eubank intimates that we might learn a lesson from his story, and I suspect that he means this in the sense of a warning lest recent Western policies turn detente into appeasement in the Munich sense. The question I want to raise is: Does the analogy hold?

## I.

United States policy toward the Soviet Union is "one-sided appeasement," "phony detente." Thus spake, recently, George Meany, one of our foremost self-appointed experts on foreign affairs.[1] But the criticism is neither limited to him nor is it recent. Over the last couple of years the general trend among experts in international politics has been going in the same direction, and some statesmen as well as scholars drew the Munich parallel as early as the end of World War II. Thus Truman, in his memoirs, tells us how the appeasement of the Thirties was present in his mind at the outbreak of the Korean War: "I recalled some earlier instances: Manchuria, Ethiopia, Austria. I remember how each time that the democracies failed to act it had encouraged the aggressor to go ahead. Communism was acting in Korea just as Hitler, Mussolini and the Japanese had acted earlier. . . . If this was to go unchallenged it would mean a third world war."[2] And listen to the voice of the great anti-appeaser himself, Winston Churchill, telling us in *his* memoirs: "If we add the United States to Britain and France; if we change the name of the potential aggressor; if we substitute the United Nations for the League of Nations, the Atlantic Ocean for the English Channel, and the world for Europe, the argument is not necessarily without its application today."[3]

Still, history knows wrong parallels. As a political scientist I want to go a bit into definitions and concepts, trying to apply them to longer periods of time. We political scientists are perhaps overly inclined to make theories and develop models for what to the historian is a unique flux of events, but our analogy problem seems to point up the need to clarify our thinking by putting into the general context of international relations such concepts as detente and appeasement. Otherwise they remain mere fighting terms that reflect conflicting attitudes and are used in the service of clashing movements and ideologies.

The political science approach tries to generalize and distinguish types of policies and attitudes that might apply to entire historical periods and whole systems of international relations. Detente and appeasement seem to me to denote behavior patterns of international actors that can be used in what has been called "conflict theory." There they can be placed into a continuum of conflict attitudes ranging all the way from aggressivity over intransigence or "standpattism" to readiness for conciliation and compromise, that is, detente, moving from there to appeasement in the sense of making unilateral concessions, hence to joining the stronger side in a conflict in hopes to share in the spoils, finally to unconditional surrender. It seems to me that, within this spectrum of behavior-patterns, three are of particular in-

terest for our discussion: First, "standpattism" in the sense
of irreconcilability, unwillingness to change a status even to
the slightest degree, defense of one's claimed rights to the
utmost; second, detente readiness in the sense of Eubank's
definition, that is, trying to arrive at rapprochement
through mutual understanding and reciprocity in concessions; third, appeasement, not in its original meaning of detente readiness but in that of a readiness—perhaps in order
to arrive at genuine detente—to make unilateral concessions to one who cannot be appeased; one here tries to
satisfy, or satiate, an unsatiable actor. Mr. Eubank refers to
this as merely the "popular meaning" of the term, but I
think it has by now become the general and generally accepted one.

## II.

Santayana once warned that those who do not learn from
history are condemned to repeat it. But the question is:
What lesson must be learned? Parallels are justified only
when situations are essentially alike. Looking backward at
the history of international constellations, one finds situations that are, so-to-speak, tailor-made for appeasement.
There are multiple units in a more or less balanced system.
Then one of the units begins to aspire to hegemony. This
confronts the others with the problem of how to react: Try
to resist and defeat the expansionist policies of the would-
be hegemony power; join and share in the spoils; deflect it
toward other potential victims; or try to appease it through
unilateral concessions. We find all of these alternatives long
before we meet them in the face of Nazi expansionism. We
may go back as far as ancient Greece, with the city states
confronting Philip of Macedonia's policy of hegemony. Listen to the warnings of Demosthenes: "We look on while the
man grows greater, because everyone has made up his
mind to profit by the time during which his neighbor is
being ruined, and nobody acts or cares for the safety of the
Hellenes."[4] Some city states thought of organizing a defen-

sive alliance with the old, no longer expansionist opponent, Persia, but only half-heartedly, since this ran counter to all traditional policy.[5] This reminds one of the equally half-hearted efforts on the part of the Western powers to negotiate with Stalin in 1939. And the attitude of the Persians was likewise one of indecision. According to Werner Jaeger, it seemed from their point of view "better to let them [the Greeks and Macedonians] wear each other down than to attempt any further intervention in these affairs."[6] The parallel to Stalin's calculations when concluding his pact with Hitler is obvious. The entire *Third Philippic* reads like Churchill in 1938 with its anxious concern to convince fellow Athenians that what they called peace was no peace: "But if any man supposes this to be peace which will enable Philip to master all else and attack you last, he is a madman."

The role of appeasement and non-appeasement emerges most prominently in the modern state system with its balance of power policies. This system, for centuries, was one of balances neglected, defended, destroyed, restored. It was characterized time and again by the emergence of a power that would try to overthrow the balance and establish its hegemony over all of Europe, whether it was Spain, or, later, France (twice, under Louis XIV and Napoleon), or still later, possibly also twice, Germany. In such instances, whenever it was too late to frustrate the would-be hegemonic power through other means, a war of the "Grand Coalition," under British (and, since World War I, United States) leadership was required to restore the balance. Appeasement, then as in the Thirties, constituted a "wrong" policy under viewpoints of the interests of the non-hegemonic powers. Thus, appeasement may be defined as a policy ignoring (or being ignorant of) what balance policy requires. What is required, and what must be avoided, has always been expressed most forcefully by leaders of the nation that for centuries was the "holder of the balance," from Bolingbroke to Churchill. Let us listen to Churchill again:

> For hundreds of years the foreign policy of England has been
> to oppose the strongest, most aggressive, most dominating
> power on the Continent. . . . It would have been tempting to
> join with the stronger and share the fruits of his conquest.
> However, we always took the hardest course, joined with the
> less strong powers . . . and thus defeated the Continental
> military tyrant whoever he was, whatever nation he led.[7]

Often it was appeasement policy that made the subsequent
war of the Grand Coalition inevitable, as in the Thirties,
when, I believe, one could have had it cheaper if one had
acted forcefully against Mussolini in 1935.

Is there, then, no alternative except appeasement and intransigence, no role of detente and genuine rapprochement? It depends on the international situation of a given
period. Vienna, after Napoleon's attempt to establish
French hegemony in Europe, had restored a balance that,
despite tensions, local wars, and hostile alliances, functioned for almost one hundred years. In 1919 one had tried
to replace an unorganized balance system by institutionaliz-
ing the balance through collective security under the
League of Nations, an effort that failed. Yet there was in
the Twenties a policy that succeeded for a while in establishing a balance in Western Europe, specifically between
France and Germany. Eubank's paper gives the impression
that there had been a thoroughgoing failure of detente
throughout the entire interwar period, attributable, chiefly,
to German intransigence. But there was, after all, Locarno,
which had been arrived at through Briand's and
Stresemann's policies of mutual understanding, and which
lasted for a number of years, based as it was on mutual
concessions (with Germany recognizing the West-European
status created at Versailles—in particular the loss of
Alsace-Lorraine, and the French making concessions in regard to reparations). Admittedly, it was a shaky detente,
because of the irreconcilables on both sides, such as the
Poincarés and the *Deutschnationale,* who, having prevented
detente prior to Locarno, put an end to it when depression

set in and nationalism rose on both sides. But I submit that one cannot place into the same flux of development the period before and after 1933. With Hitler's rise to power, there entered an entirely new element: striving for hegemony. Even the German nationalists' and militarists' aims were limited as compared with Hitler's. Thus, whatever, under a detente policy, the Western powers might have granted a still mildly revisionist Germany ("mild" as compared with Nazi objectives), they instead, foolishly, set out to grant an unappeasable regime. Austen Chamberlain's efforts were for genuine detente, while those of Neville Chamberlain amounted to appeasement.

## III.

Let us now turn to our analogy problem and ask: What has been the role of detente, standpattism, and appeasement in the postwar period? It is my thesis that the present is *not* comparable to the Thirties. Again, our assessment is predicated upon the general international system. That emerging from World War II turned out to be a bipolar system where two superpowers, organized in power blocs, have opposed each other but so far have been deterred from risking all-out war by the mutually suicidal nature of the nuclear weapon. Being antagonists in most everything—in doctrine, way of life, internal system—the Soviets and the Western bloc, leaders as well as publics, were inclined to view the respective adversary as bent on world hegemony, the West suspecting a Communist "world conspiracy" to destroy the "free world," the East convinced that "capitalist imperialism" was out to wipe out "socialism." Under such symmetrically opposed views (one the mirror-image of the other) any concession, any ever-so-moderate effort to lessen tension, would, on both sides, be considered appeasement—and this quite understandably, after the experience of the Thirties; only standpattism, not yielding an inch, seemed to protect one's security. Thus, at the time of the Cuban missile crisis, both Kennedy and Khrushchev were accused by their respective intransigents of having given in to the opponent. (The Chinese even used the term Munich, and it is likely that Khrushchev's subsequent fall from power was due to the intransigent element in the Politbureau.)[8]

Such mutual, mirror-image types of recrimination must make one pause and ask whether the truth is not in the middle. Both images may well be wrong. That is, instead of both sides, or at least one of them, being expansionist and ultimately bent on world domination, in reality, with their rational insight into the irrationality of the use of all-out force in the nuclear age, both sides are defensive-minded, i.e., interested primarily in the maintenance and defense of the status quo that had resulted from the war.

It is not my intention here to warm up the controversy about the origins of the cold war into which those mutual suspicions and recriminations led the two power blocs. In my opinion they were neither in Soviet expansionism or Communist world conspiracy nor in U.S. imperialism but, rather, in what I call the "security dilemma" of nations, that is, their mutual fears and suspicions that the other side might turn aggressive. Admittedly, the Soviets' moving into what Hitler had presented Stalin on a silver platter through invasion and subsequent defeat, namely, control of Eastern Europe, looked like unappeasable expansionism to some in the West, but might it not, from the Soviet viewpoint, be considered as building a defensive belt around a much invaded country, particularly when the Americans engaged in what looked to them as encirclement, through troops stationed all along the Iron Curtain and bases scattered across the globe from Thule to Okinawa; by building blocs and alliances and, above all, rearming the former chief enemy, the Germans? In a situation of "security dilemma," whatever is done for precaution and defense by one side, is liable to be interpreted as offensive by the other.

However this may have been, it is clear even from what happened during the cold war that both sides had come to recognize the lines of deepest military penetration of their forces at the end of the war by and large as the lines demarcating their respective power spheres, and that these might be crossed only at the risk of a war nobody wanted. Bipolarity thus meant stalemate, a balance of sorts, and consequently, a mutual, if tacit agreement not to interfere in the sphere of the other. Even at the height of the cold war, this policy of restraint could be observed at the time of the East German uprising, the Hungarian revolution, the invasion of Czechoslovakia, and on the Soviet side whenever, during one of the perennial crises over Berlin, a Stalin or Khrushchev refrained from trying to take over a city that, geographically, was located deep within their sphere.

In such a situation, must we have standpattism with all its risks of crisis and confrontation, its non-recognition policies, its intransigence in regard to ever so utopian legal claims, its arms races and competition for influence in ever so remote areas? Or are there chances for rapprochement and genuine detente? Standpattism, as we have seen, is the correct policy in the face of an adversary's hegemonial and expansionist policies, whereas detente is possible—and does *not* involve appeasement—when both sides are basically status-quo-minded.

One could not "do business" with Hitler by trying to establish lines of demarcation or spheres of influence. One can, with proper precautions, I believe, do business of this sort with Soviet leaders. I am aware that to recognize this possibility goes against the grain of those who still believe in the unalterable final goal of Communism to conquer the world, and this belief, ironically, is bolstered by the fact that Communist leaders, in order to maintain their ideological credibility, are inclined to emphasize those goals (Khrushchev's "We will bury you," etc.), although such objectives belong to the category of ultimate but presently unrealizable ideals, while a Hitler, dissembling his real objectives, could deceive the world for years with his famous "peace speeches." But if one wants to see the difference between genuine world-revolutionary involvement and one-single-nation policy one should compare what Lenin and other early Bolsheviks were expecting and aiming at with what Stalin and his successors actually were striving for. Thus, Bukharin, in 1917, declared: "The task of the Bolshevist Party is the universal assistance of international revolution," and in March 1919, Lenin foresaw the imminent foundation of an "all-world federative Soviet Republic." About the same time Zinoviev declared: "Now, as these lines are being written, there exist already three Soviet Republics, in Russia, Hungary, and Bavaria. Nobody will be surprised if when these lines are published, there will be, not three, but six or even a greater number. . . ."[9] But by the time the article appeared, the number had been reduced to exactly one. Stalin drew the only realistic conclusion: to build socialism in that one country and subordinate everything else, including the fate of foreign revolutions and the function of foreign Communist parties, to the survival of the Soviet Union. After Stalin's victory over Hitler the new, and favorable, status quo[10] was the one hence to be defended and protected, and in view of the new threat to Soviet security perceived, rightly or wrongly, at her Eastern flank, Stalin's successors, by and large, have maintained this non-revisionist, defensive policy toward the West. Thus both sides, at least for the time being, had accepted the postwar distribution and balance of power.

IV.

There was, however, one flaw in this situation. While, basically, the new status quo in Europe was recognized by East and West, there was the exception of the German question. West Germany, backed by her allies, refused to give up her claim to "reunification in freedom" (that is, inclusion of East Germany in the Western sphere) and to recognize the new boundary with Poland (that is, give up claims to the Eastern territories), which meant non-recognition of the GDR, of the Oder-Neisse line, etc. But a balance is never stable when a major actor is wedded to revising it, and thus general detente was still hamstrung by intransigence and confrontation.

But stalemate, even though acknowledged by both sides, must not necessarily be perpetuated. If both sides are determined to seek accommodation, stalemate may be used as a starting point for loosening up a situation. When, in the late Sixties, Bonn became ready to recognize the post-war European status, and Moscow was ready to accept a strong and rearmed Western-aligned Federal Republic, the major obstacles in the way of detente were removed, and what is now known as *Ostpolitik* could be inaugurated.

I would like ever so briefly to place *Ostpolitik* into the context of our discussion. Those who were "present at the creation" of the Federal Republic and the cold war, the Achesons, the former U.S. High Commissioners in West Germany, together with the West German opposition (and, I am sure, in accordance with mirror-image reservations within the Politbureau) have called that policy "surrender." The fact that, once more, "Munich"-type charges originated from extremists on both sides must make us pause. *Ostpolitik*, in my judgment, merely meant the formal recognition of a *de facto* status created right after, and as a consequence of, World War II. The West accepted nothing that had not, in fact, existed for a quarter of a century. "Nothing is given up," said Willy Brandt at the signing of the Moscow Treaty, "that was not gambled away long ago." No territory changed hands, nor were there changes in political alignments; the overall strategic or political balance was not affected. But—if I may quote from another article of mine—"if West Germany now, through *Ostpolitik*, signalized that she was ready finally to make peace with the East on the basis of defeat in World War II, realizing that Germans had to pay for the excesses committed by a criminal regime, it did mean creating a new basis for peace and stability in Europe."[11] And even if one considers the legitimization of the GDR and its regime and of Eastern boundaries as a Western concession, it was not a unilateral one. There was reciprocity in the Soviet guarantee of the status of West Berlin as a Western unit, of free access to it, of improved personal contacts between East and West in regard to travel, visiting, etc. That there was mutuality of concessions, a genuine give and take, can be seen from the great reluctance of the East German government to accede to the agreements (Ulbricht had to go); it is still the one that places the greatest obstacles in the path of detente.[12]

Three place-names which have become symbols for policies in the interwar period may serve to clarify: Munich, Rapallo, Locarno. That *Ostpolitik* did not involve a Munich (in the sense of a unilateral give-away) I hope to have shown. What about Rapallo? Rapallo, the place where, in 1922, Germans and Soviets agreed to establish diplomatic relations, has ever since been used as shorthand for German-Russian rapprochement, if not German "betrayal of the West."[13] Hans Morgenthau perceives such a risk in Soviet detente efforts now.[14] I cannot agree. There is nobody in any responsible position in West Germany today who would be seducible this way and advocate giving up Western ties for an Eastern orientation. Short of a rise to power of a neo-Nazi group or else the Communist Party, something rather inconceivable now, this is simply not in the cards. As for the Soviets, they must, after all, have learned something from the failure of the Stalin-Hitler Pact. I doubt whether they would welcome as an ally even a Communized Germany, a unit that would duplicate China at their Western flank (not to speak of the fact that such a German reorientation could only be had in return for reunification, and how would that affect the other bloc members?). Therefore I would rather draw the parallel of Locarno. Locarno, as we have seen, meant German recognition of the post-World War I status in Western Europe and thus initiated Franco-German detente. *Ostpolitik* involves an "Eastern Locarno," that Eastern Locarno the German intransigents had refused in the Twenties when they dreamed of chopping up or gobbling up Poland. Now the frontier with Poland has been recognized. The way is thus open to closer personal, economic, and cultural relations with the nations of the East, which, so it seems to me, have a better chance of internal liberalization this way than through a continuation of a Western policy of ostracism.

But the latter tendency, the emotionalism of intransigence and hostility, is never far below the surface of detente. Listen to what that great foreign policy expert, Congressman John Rooney, had to say when invited to attend a reception for visiting Polish party chief Gierek:

> Not only do I decline this invitation to honor the No. 1 representative of atheistic Red Russian Communism in Poland, that stooge of Moscow who is the enemy of His Eminence Stefan Cardinal Wyscynski, but I resent the invitation.[15]

Even though, at this point, statements like this one may be rhetoric, they may make a difference. Political atmosphere does count. A much ridiculed "spirit," such as the "spirit of Thoiry," in the Twenties, the "spirit of Camp David," etc., may become conducive to accommodation, while a spirit of constant suspicion—to be distinguished from wholesome caution and watchfulness—may become self-fulfilling prophecy. Euphoria, on the other hand, is no great help either. What is needed in creating and maintaining an atmosphere of detente is calm, down-to-earth assessment of the given situation and its opportunities, if any.

. . . . . .

The greatest threat to detente I perceive today lies with the military and its supporters on both sides. Detente policy has been attacked for alleged neglect of so-called defense and security interests. I would criticize SALT negotiations and related policies rather for having achieved almost nothing and, by not calling a halt to the insane arms race with its piling one new weapons system upon the other, for increasing not only the danger of the ultimate blowup of the world but also the more imminent one of bankrupting the industrialized countries—apparently first the Western ones. It would be truly absurd if, without having had a conscious policy of the sort, the Soviets (and/or the Chinese) would this way inherit the Western world. As long as second-strike and overkill capacities are maintained, even radical reduction of armaments would not imply appeasement or surrender; on the contrary, it constitutes, in my opinion, the only way to genuine detente among the superpowers. I am critical of Mr. Kissinger's efforts not because of his detente policies toward Moscow and Peking or his efforts to arrive at Near Eastern detente through establishing some sort of peace, or at least mutual toleration, between Israel and the Arabs, but because of insufficient efforts in the area of weapons control, as well as continued non-detente policies in South-East Asia and even open intervention in countries like Chile.[16]

In this utterly inflammable world of ours, all of us, whether West or East, North or South, are bound to go down or survive together. Trying to reduce tension so as to be able jointly to meet the really great global challenges —the food and resources crisis, the energy crisis, the threatening destruction of the biosphere—is, I submit, the only path to survival.

## NOTES

1. *The New York Times*, October 2, 1974.

2. Harry S. Truman, *Memoirs* (New York: Doubleday, 1958), Vol. 2, p. 333.

3. Winston Churchill, *The Second World War* (Boston: Houghton Mifflin, 1948), Vol. I (*The Gathering Storm*), p. 211.

4. From the *Third Philippic*.

5. A.W. Pickard-Cambridge, *Demosthenes and the Last Days of Greek Freedom, 384-322 B.C.* (New York: Putnam, 1914), pp. 340f.

6. Werner Jaeger, *Demosthenes* (Berkeley: University of California Press, 1938), p. 181.

7. Churchill, *op. cit.*, pp. 207f.

8. For more on this as well as other aspects of appeasement see John H. Herz, "The Relevancy and Irrelevancy of Appeasement," *Social Research*, Vol. 31, No. 3, 1964, pp. 296ff.

9. For sources of these quotations and further details see John H. Herz: *Political Realism and Political Idealism* (Chicago: University of Chicago Press, 1951, paper edition, 1973), especially pp. 88ff.

10. Comparable, perhaps, to the one achieved by Bismarck after his victory over the French, which rendered German foreign policy for about twenty years one of non-revisionist status-quo policy.

11. John H. Herz, section on *Germany* in Gregory Henderson, Richard Ned Lebow, and John G. Stoessinger, eds.; *Divided Nations in a Divided World* (New York: McKay, 1974), p. 17. See this section also for an overall discussion and analysis of *Ostpolitik*.

12. As for mutuality of concessions, there is a story of Soviet negotiator Abrassimov having remarked, after signing the Quadripartite Agreement on Berlin: "Now they will liquidate me."

13. The original Rapallo agreement, of course, did not imply this. It provided for the establishment of diplomatic relations between Germany and the Soviet Union, implying a certain assertion of independence on Germany's part but no realignment. In this respect, rather than comparing it with what happened in 1970, it might be compared with the establishment of Bonn-Moscow relations by Adenauer in 1955.

14. See, e.g., his "The United States and Europe in a Decade of Detente," in Wolfram F. Hanrieder, ed.: *The United States and Western Europe* (Cambridge, Mass.: Winthrop, 1974), p. 7.

15. *The New York Times*, October 3, 1974.

16. That arms control and arms reduction are intimately connected with detente, and detente, in turn, with the approach to the global economic and environment problems mentioned in the last paragraph of this article is explained in more detail in my book *Staatenwelt und Weltpolitik* (Hoffmann und Campe Verlag, Hamburg, 1974), in particular *Einleitung* (Introduction) and chapter 9. I would also like to refer the reader to recent elucidations of this theme by Senator Walter F. Mondale in his article

"Beyond Detente: Toward International Economic Security,"
*Foreign Affairs*, Vol. 53, No. 1, October, 1974. Some of his remarks
come very close to the core of this discussion:

> Certainly detente is important. The gains in East-West rela-
> tions must be consolidated on a realistic basis; negotiations on
> strategic arms, the European Security Conference and the
> questions of force levels in Europe must be pursued. . . . But
> international economic policy is now our top external
> challenge. . . . We must seize the opportunities presented by
> detente . . . to deal effectively with our economic problems, or
> the progress we have made toward a more secure world may
> be undone. In the 1920's there was also a version of detente,
> symbolized by the Treaty of Locarno, and at the same time an
> emerging depression. When the nations of the world failed to
> cooperate to deal with the depression, its consequences rapidly
> unraveled the elements of that detente, and in the end
> economic collapse contributed mightily both to the emergence
> of grave threats from Germany and Japan and to the paralysis
> of other nations, including the United States, in the face of
> those threats (pp.lf.,6).

My only reservation concerns the use of the term "economic,"
which is actually meant to comprise all the great global questions,
from population explosion and its effects to the threat of environmental destruction.

# DISCUSSION—OCT. 25

RENÉ ALBRECHT-CARRIÉ, *Columbia University*

Having heard various interpretations of the meaning of detente, I am inclined to agree with Abba Eban, who recently bemoaned the fact that in the English language we have to use a French word which lends itself to very different interpretations. I think the point has already been made that a distinction has to be drawn between detente and appeasement. Appeasement may lead to detente, but this is a very different animal.

KLAUS PRINGSHEIM, *McMaster University, Canada*

As one who lived in Europe during this particular time and has some vague recollections of what took place then, it seems to me that the word "detente" was not much in use in the middle thirties. As a matter of fact, the predominant word would have been appeasement, and I share the misgivings of Professor Albrecht-Carrié about the applicability of using the two words interchangeably.

Q. RENÉ ALBRECHT-CARRIÉ, *Columbia University*

Professor Eubank's paper has given us an excellent presentation of British foreign policy via-à-vis Germany. The British were mainly interested in a relaxation of tension —detente—with Germany. And the record of the British effort would make an interesting story worth telling. But I consider that the record of the Franco-German relationship, especially during the 1920's, is a much better illustration of detente than the Anglo-German relationship later on. Would you like to comment on this?

A. KEITH EUBANK, *The City University of New York*

I agree that in the relationship between France and Germany there was more tension than between Great Britain and Germany. There is very definitely a whole other side to the story of Germany and France. This is something which should be studied when the French government allows us to get in and look at these documents. Apparently they are not going to be published. I emphasized the British because they were, I felt, somewhat similar to what Mr. Kissinger was doing in being very eager for this [detente], and very much intent on trying to pacify and quiet things down.

As I pointed out, I think the interesting thing is that behind it all, to a certain extent, was a purely budgetary feeling on Chamberlain's part, that if we can calm things down, business will improve and taxes will drop.

Q. PETER BAUER, *VWD German Economic News Service*

I totally agree with Professor Herz that a distinction must be drawn between the pre-1933 period and the period 1933-1939. Do you think, Professor Herz, that a policy of detente between France and Germany could have succeeded?

A. JOHN H. HERZ, *The City University of New York*

If the depression had not happened, and if in consequence Hitler had not risen to power, I think the situation would have been similar to that in the twenties, with a certain chance of continuing detente, because there was an appeasable power. In my mind, Germany up to 1933, although revisionist, especially as regards her eastern boundary, was appeasable through certain territorial concessions in regard to her eastern boundaries. Had this been agreed upon, without a Hitler, then I think we might have had a chance of ongoing detente.

But the point I would like to emphasize is the complete difference between the pre-1933 and the post-1933 period. Before 1933 you have a power which in principle is appeasable, is amenable to talking about mutual concessions. The government you had in power from 1933 was not appeasable, despite the dissimulation in Hitler's self-styled "peace speeches" at the very beginning—before he had a chance to rearm.

Q. KLAUS PRINGSHEIM, *McMaster University, Canada*

It appears to me that the impression of a great many

people who were reading newspapers and editorials in the 1930's was that detente was not an exercise in relaxing tension, but that it was more of an exercise in strategic stalling, because the rumors seemed to be that Mr. Hitler was building a very strong army, air force, and navy, and that the British had not the wherewithal to counteract the armaments of Hitler. Therefore, detente, or rather appeasement, as I think we would have been inclined to call it, was a desire to stall until budgetary and political measures could be taken in Britain and other allied countries to bring them up to a point where they could speak with greater authority in resisting the bonds of Mr. Hitler.

A. KEITH EUBANK, *The City University of New York*

Unfortunately, that did not really become the case until about the time that Mr. Hitler was going to bring down the whole thing on their heads, from what I have seen. Now there may undoubtedly be material back in the Public Record Office which may show that, but certainly there was no stalling on MacDonald's part. He was never intent on doing that. Baldwin was not very eager too, and the stalling really becomes very apparent in 1938 when Chamberlain speaks to the chiefs of staff and they say we are not ready for war now and you must give us time.

There is not, in the material that I have seen, a conscious playing for time until just before the end, when they finally realize that this policy of detente or appeasement in which they got the words mixed up—that is the reason why in their minds the two phrases were very often confused and mixed up—it was not until the end when all of this is about to come tumbling down and they come up against the harsh realities, that there is a clearly discernible policy. Now there may have been some before that, but it is not apparent until 1938, when suddenly the crisis is upon them and then they say we have got to stall, and that is one of the basic reasons for the Munich agreement—definitely an intention to stall.

The other evidence that he [Chamberlain] was told by his professionals was that we can not cut it now, and have to stall. Very definitely they were doing it then. Earlier I have not found the evidence. It may be there, buried.

**Q. STEVEN WARNECKE,** *The City University of New York*

Professor Eubank, you suggested that Chamberlain's position showed lack of judgment and weakness. However, it might be possible to argue that there was a very sensible element in British policy toward Hitler—at least from the British understanding of the difference between the United Kingdom's interests and those of France. I would like to know if a full understanding of the British position on detente with Nazi Germany would require some reference to British global policy between the First and Second World Wars. If it does then I think it might be possible to support the argument that the British only saw Europe as one part of a larger global mosaic within which Western Europe was one component, whereas for the French, Europe was much more important because of their geographic proximity to Germany.

**A. KEITH EUBANK,** *The City University of New York*

Very definitely. That is a very important point which perhaps should be stressed. The British had a lot of headaches and problems, and Chamberlain's policies, many of the ones for which he has been denounced, become much more logical when you see what the Commonwealth governments were saying, and the problems Britain faced in the Far East—where they were wrestling with the Japanese and probably not getting the help that they wanted from the United States.

Clearly the British had a worldwide problem and the French did not. You are absolutely right that the British had a lot of other headaches.

**Q. STEPHEN XYDIS,** *The City University of New York*

In his analogy between the post-war period and the pre-war detente has Professor Herz for some reason avoided the basic fact that in one case you had a relationship between victors and vanquished, whereas in the other very important case you have a quarrel between allies as soon as the goal of the coalition was achieved. That seems to me to be a big difference. You have there a symmetry between the two participants and the conflict. That makes a difference, the mirror image because you have a symmetry there, two allies that quarrel when victory is achieved, whereas, of course, the other case is between a defeated country and victors.

A. JOHN H. HERZ, *The City University of New York*

I think that this is a very good point.

STEPHEN XYDIS, *The City University of New York*

I think that is a big difference.

JOHN H. HERZ, *The City University of New York*

I agree. It reflects something deeper, namely that you have now what we call a bipolar situation. You now have two worlds, and only two worlds. In former times you had a multiple system where one of several powers could try to establish hegemony. Then appeasement was the wrong policy. But if we have only two, and the two are deterred from going to war by the nuclear factor, then, to my mind, it does not make too much sense to talk about appeasement because the insatiability element is no longer relevant.

Q. JAY STONE, *Ph.D. Candidate, The City University of New York*

May I address myself to the question of the partners involved in detente? The question was raised that at the end of World War II we were faced by two equal allies, whereas at the end of World War I one ally was obviously a defeated power. Is this perhaps a wrong direction from which to approach the whole question of entente—if indeed that was inferred? It seems to me that the most important point in the analysis of any entente situation is that of understanding objectives, and that is reading whether the partner you are dealing with is actually one involved in status quo policy or in one of hegemony. This is what we really must address ourselves to in dealing with the Soviet Union as a prospective entente partner.

A. JOHN H. HERZ, *The City University of New York*

Professor Eubank, at one point, I believe, you mentioned entente and not detente. One should clearly distinguish between the two. You have detente as a consequence of a conflict situation, as an attempt to lessen tension or conflict. Entente signifies much more than that, namely, friendship. Nobody would talk about the possibility of entente between the Soviet Union and the United States unless one is an inveterate optimist or utopian. Entente could be applied to the *entente cordiale* between France and Britain, but only because there was at the same time, as Professor Eubank also mentioned, the conflict between the two on the one hand, and the rise of Germany on the other hand.

A. KEITH EUBANK, *The City University of New York*

There was also a very definite fear of the possibility of certain conflict between the two. There are pathetic reports from the naval commanders who had to deal with the Newfoundland fishermen whom the French fishermen confronted off the coast of Newfoundland in the summer before this agreement; they felt there was going to be an actual shooting war between the fishermen.

There were other things in the colonial quarrels that kept the foreign offices unhappy. So friendship did ultimately evolve out of this, and I think it is one of the strange things that it did, but there were still people who felt it was a little bit odd. The real friend was Germany and that is the one they wanted really to go back to throughout the twenties and the thirties. There was a desire that there be real friendship and similar interests; we somehow must have this detente which will lead to appeasement. Things will calm down and we will get the settlement that we ought to have gotten.

PAUL RIEBENFELD, *Institute for Mediterranean Affairs*

It would seem that the treatment of Hitler's Germany in the thirties was an anachronistic carry-over of an attitude which had developed as a reaction to Weimar Germany. We probably should divide the issue of ideology in pre-war Great Britain into two time periods. Until 1938 one dealt with grievances which had been largely accepted as justified, almost since Versailles. Their correction seemed overdue and held the hope of defusing the aggressive character of Nazism. By the time of the *Anschluss* it was clear that the desired revision of the Peace Treaty could be achieved peacefully, and that was the time, at the very latest, when it should have been recognized that Hitler's intentions could not be appeased. Both the style and the objects of German policy were those of *Mein Kampf*, not aiming at revision, but in greed far surpassing the wildest dreams of Imperial Germany. There were no concessions in the power of Britain and France to make which could have bought off Hitler.

Secondly, when dealing with the Soviet Union, we deal with a totalitarian power compared with which Nazi Germany was an open society. Can you really write off, as Professor Herz has done, the issue of ideology to which a totalitarian society is tuned, when talking about its policy? Ostensible policy changes are possible from day to day, but they may be meaningless. This was the case regarding the German-Polish non-aggression treaty of January 1934, which no German took seriously.

I remember when I arrived in England in 1936, having come originally from Germany. I was sure that I understood more about German intentions than any Englishman, whatever his position, and events unfortunately justified my impatience with what I considered British obtuseness. I was a very young man, and certainly no Sakharov or Solzhenitsyn. Today these two Soviet experts, with tremendous courage, are warning us constantly about the spirit underlying the course of Soviet foreign policy. I, for one, have more confidence in their view than I have in the analyses of Western Kremlinologists, not to mention the pronouncements of Soviet diplomats.

The other day, at a conference in Washington on detente

at which, by the way, Professors Schwab, Friedlander, and Rustow were also present, I heard a Russian intellectual, Lev Navrozov, make a disturbing comment. He said that, to him, the decision of the Soviet leadership to permit Jewish emigration indicates only one thing: they intend to catch up with these Jews in Israel eventually. Otherwise, it was too much out of character. Well, the Jewish situation is an extraordinary one, and I hope one need not jump to such drastic conclusions.

But I would like to put in a caveat on the whole issue of ideology and foreign relations. When dealing with a closed society, we cannot afford any wishful thinking.

This brings me to a particular aspect of British policy which has not been mentioned by Professor Eubank, but which was of the utmost importance. I refer to the role of public opinion, which was so powerfully demonstrated in Britain after the occupation of Prague. Such words as detente or appeasement, though without precise meaning, are code words capable of triggering deep emotions and expectations. If public opinion feels deceived, as in Britain after March 15, 1939, the resulting backlash can sweep away government policies and governments—even government systems.

Public opinion was controlling British foreign policy during the summer of 1939, until the morning of September 3rd. All documents, all memoirs show that Chamberlain, until the last moment, long after the invasion of Poland, hoped for some mediation or agreement that might prevent war. When Arthur Greenwood rose in Parliament on the evening of September 2nd, cheered not only by his own party but by the Conservatives—Leopold Amery shouting to him, "Speak for England"—Chamberlain was still hesitating, and the Cabinet under the spur of popular fury forced his hand later that evening. During the preceding months, when Dr. Wohltat and other German emissaries were rotating guests in London, any attempts at buying peace, such as a $5 billion loan and the promise of colonies for Germany, were bound to fail, on account of the revulsion of British public opinion, even if Hitler had been amenable to compromise. Whatever the British government planned in continuation of attempted appeasement had to remain ineffective after Prague.

The power of public opinion is not unknown in this country. Whether we think as historians or political scientists, we must be warned, and must warn, of the possible effects of a backlash of public opinion if it becomes unduly disappointed. Public opinion takes large swings and changes much more irrationally than government policy. Such thinking provides the only reason that makes some sense in trying to explain why Dr. Kissinger during the October war was so solicitous of the Soviet Union's reputation, maintaining that their behavior this time was more moderate than in May and June of 1967, and insisting that the Russian attempt at involving additional Arab states in the war and encouraging the oil embargo did not transgress the spirit of detente. Rather doubtful propositions—but perhaps seen as necessary if detente was not to collapse there and then.

My last point deals with the question of rearmament, to which no place was given by Professor Eubank. That the country had been overtaken by the speed of German rearmament was most decisive in determining British policy. The Labour Party, which was hostile to everything the Nazis represented, and most vociferous in its opposition to appeasement, especially after the outbreak of the Spanish Civil War, nevertheless consistently refused to vote for an adequate defense program. Such was the lack of enthusiasm for an arms build-up that Prime Minister Baldwin confessed in 1936 to having deceived the electorate regarding the comparative state of German and British weapons manufacture in order to win reelection. The British public simply refused to understand that any arrangement with Germany required a strong defense posture, and the government gave no lead.

Without going into details, I would say this certainly

seems most relevant to the present situation, when America is falling back in armaments; when the Soviet Union is building a Blue Water navy; when we are producing about 800 tanks a year against the Russians building over 8000; when the supply of planes, tanks, and munitions to one small ally drains our inventories dangerously. How, for instance, can we conduct a policy which might draw Egypt into the Western camp, if it would take us eight years to replace the Soviet equipment of its military forces? I do not say that Egypt's policy would necessarily change were things different. But it seems to me that these questions are of tremendous importance if we want to draw a realistic parallel and learn what lessons the past holds for us today.

HENRY FRIEDLANDER, *The City College of New York*

I happen not to agree with the assertion originally made by Professor Herz that 1933 was an important date. I happen to feel that the choice of the victors at Versailles was to do one of two things: either to imitate the Congress of Vienna's treatment of post-Napoleonic France by admitting defeated Germany to the peace conference as an equal with almost no loss in power and territory (in other words, to restore her to the position from which she attempted to grasp world domination, using here Fritz Fischer's *Griff nach der Weltmacht* concept), or to treat her as did the Allies in the Second World War (in other words, to occupy and divide her).

It seems to me that these were the only two choices. When the Allies chose another approach somewhat in between these two extremes, they had to deal with a revanchist and irredentist Germany. Thus Germany from 1919 on—not only after 1933—demanded revisions which the victors could not grant. If you read the statements on foreign policy, for example on the Baltic issued by Ebert and Hitler, you will find that on these issues, devoid of ideology, they only differed in the shrillness of their rhetoric.

DANKWART A. RUSTOW, *The City University of New York*

May I briefly comment on Professor Friedlander's remark. There are some conferences where everybody agrees, there are some conferences where the organizers and all the performers agree, and then any disagreement comes from the audience, and happily, this is a conference where some of the organizers disagree with some of the performers. I think I am perhaps for the first time in my life coming around to the position proposed by Professor Himmelfarb, namely, that history holds no lessons. I have always thought that history was the only thing we could learn lessons from. What else would we be learning it from, except things that actually happened? But perhaps I would rephrase Professor Himmelfarb's proposition and simply say that to every tenable lesson from history, there are at least a dozen tenuous ones, and the most tenuous one I have heard recently is that the only difference between Friedrich Ebert and Adolf Hitler was one of rhetoric. There was a difference in rhetoric, but there were other differences too —and this implies no particular admiration for Ebert. We can be critical of a number of people in different degrees, but to obliterate the degrees of difference or fundamental differences and reduce them to one of mere rhetoric, I think is no service to historical understanding.

GERTRUDE HIMMELFARB, *The City University of New York*

The position I was describing was, of course, Oakeshott's. I am not sure I myself subscribe to it entirely, although I do agree that the lessons to be drawn from history are not always obvious or straightforward.

JOHN H. HERZ, *The City University of New York*

Permit me to comment on Professor Friedlander's statement. After the defeat of Germany I think the only realistic solution would have been to apply the parallel of Vienna. After all, France was not restored to anything looking like

Napoleon's hegemony but reduced to her former boundaries.

There were certain territorial questions where Germany
had to give in, Alsace Lorraine, for instance. That she did.
By the same token, I believe that if later one had come to
an agreement on certain concessions in regard to Danzig
and the Polish boundary, that would have been a solution
which would have been fair to Germany and to the
others—even to Poland. And so I do not agree at all with
Professor Friedlander's view that there was only the alternative of either having hegemonial though temporarily defeated Germany, or to cut up Germany completely.

**KEITH EUBANK,** *The City University of New York*

One comment that came to mind while Professor Friedlander was talking, about what they were faced with at Versailles: either a type of Vienna agreement or they could do
as we have done recently, namely, occupy it, or they could
try and do what they did, neither one or the other.

We know that, obviously, they should have approached it
in a different spirit than what they did, after the mistakes
that were made, and they decided in 1945 to occupy it. I
do like to tell my students that they would not have had as
much trouble then, with the difficulties in the 1920's, if they
had treated the Germans just like the Yankees did when
they came down and occupied us in 1865. And we learned
down there, according to my relatives, that we were defeated, and that made quite a difference when you have
been occupied by Yankees. Some of my ancestors lived
through it and it made quite an impression on them.

**Q. FRED BAUMANN,** *Ph.D.*

We have heard much talk about rhetoric today. For example, it was argued that the difference between Ebert and
Hitler was essentially one of rhetoric. We also notice from
Professor Herz' paper the contrast between his view of
comments by Khrushchev (whose statement that "we will
bury you" was dismissed pretty much as standard boiler-plate)

and his severe criticism of Congressman Rooney for a very similarly partisan comment about Prime Minister Gierek. I wonder if the double standard that I sense there is not symptomatic of the stake that we have developed in detente. Thus, the more optimistic, democratic, peaceful, and moderate regime tends to bend over backward to preserve its sense of the good faith of its partner. I wonder too, if that increased commitment (which I believe was mentioned by Professor Eubank), is not dangerous to the successful development of a reciprocal detente.

To put it in a slightly different way, Professor Herz seemed to emphasize that what made detente possible after World War II was the balance of power and the consequent standpat attitude that prevailed generally.

Now this balance seems to have led to a faith in the general stability of the system, which in turn led to a certain optimism about detente. Is not that stability precisely what is lost by the process of detente, while the desire for the success of detente continues to grow? Does not this lead to a danger for the United States, which is the more lazy, easy going, and moderate, as well as (I think one can say this legitimately) the more peace-loving regime, when it deals with a regime that exhibits, one could say, the expansiveness of the Athenian empire combined with the discipline of ancient Sparta?

A. JOHN H. HERZ, *The City University of New York*

The whole thrust of my paper was to show that detente policy is *not* a policy of unilateral concessions. The latter may, indeed, lead to a change or even an overthrow of the balance. But detente is a policy of reciprocity, of *mutual* concessions.

Can you prove to me that Kissinger's or anybody else's detente policy (This policy really started much before Kissinger; it started in the early sixties), has been a policy of unilateral western concession for which we did get nothing? If this were so, then, of course, you would be right. What I attempted to show, at least in so far as Europe is concerned, is that it involved not a change in the balance, not even a territorial change; and, second, that there was reciprocity, if you take for instance, on the one hand the recognition of the G.D.R. by the West, and on the other hand the Eastern guarantee of Berlin.

Q.  ROBERTO SOCAS, *Essex County College, N.J.*

As far as I can see, ideology in the 1930's did not play as significant a role with regard to the relations between Britain and Germany as ideology has played in the relations between the Soviet Union and the United States. I wonder if Professor Eubank would care to comment on this point?

A.  KEITH EUBANK, *The City University of New York*

There was definitely a strong ideological undercurrent. The trouble was that there were two different ideologies, and they never could get quite together. And that is, I think, the problem in detente with Mr. Kissinger and the Russians. If they are both agreed, if they can be as much as any two governments like this can be, then both are looking on detente with a certain basic agreement. Is there a basic agreement on where they are going? This I find was lacking with the British and the French.

HENRY PACHTER, *The City College of New York*

I have difficulty with the concept of insatiability or unappeasability. Is not this a relative concept? For instance, Hitler, as we know, had given orders when he occupied the Rhineland to withdraw in case there should be any resistance. Now assume the Western powers would not have told him so clearly that they would not defend Czechoslovakia—is it not reasonable to assume that without that information he might not have occupied that country?

He may have been insatiable in his desire to reconquer territory or to reoccupy colonies or what-not, to achieve hegemony, but if he had been contained by a policy of alliances, he might not have been able to follow his insatiable hunger for territory.

So what I would like to suggest is that we cannot, on the

basis of something that someone has written, or what is usually referred to as ideology, conclude that he could not have been appeased, but he could have been contained. That is to say the consequences of appeasement would not have appeared. Now, no matter what you might think about the ideology of Moscow, it seems to me quite obvious that Russian imperialism exists without ideology, that their policy in the Mediterranean, in the Middle East, is determined by geographical factors, that they would like to have an influence on Cyprus or on certain other pieces of geography and that this is quite independent from the subjective desire or satiability that they have. Let us say they are forced to live in a context of world politics, of the balance of power, they might be satiated for whatever subjective desires they might have, and whatever the ideology might prescribe. But when opportunity presents itself, they will expand their influence.

I was amazed that Professor Herz referred to the ideology as, in this case, a negative factor: there is no ideology of world conquest, and therefore, we have nothing to fear. I do not know whether this is the correct approach. The correct approach is, of course, to consider the Russian empire like every other empire that has certain congenital elements of expansionism, of security, and therefore, can only be contained if other nations also have a similar tendency and other empires also contain it.

A. KEITH EUBANK, *The City University of New York*

In reply to some of the speaker's comments, I would like to say that the idea of containment is definitely true. Hitler could have been contained by an alliance that was prepared to go to war. But that was the problem that Chamberlain was always afraid of. If you called Hitler's bluff, then you had to shoot. It would have been much worse if you bluffed and you were not ready to shoot and did not want to shoot.

As to the Rhineland, there is no evidence available that there were orders to pull back. As far as is known, there was a standing order in 1936 to resist if you encounter hostiles in Germany. The Germans were going into German territory, and if they encountered hostiles, the standing order that they had—D.C. Watt pointed this out—was to fight if you encounter hostiles.

Here public opinion came in. Public opinion was definitely a powerful factor in Britain throughout the 1920's and 1930's. Public opinion did not want another war. Yes, Hitler could have been contained. What it comes down to in the last analysis is: are we prepared to fight? The answer is no.

A. JOHN H. HERZ, *The City University of New York*

Since Professor Pachter brought my name into the discussion, may I please say a word. I do not think that I have neglected the factor of ideology. Just the opposite. The policy of appeasement neglected Nazi ideology which, as you put it, implied insatiable hunger for territory. I say that Hitler might have been contained. I remember having lived through those times, and the feeling of tragedy many of us had. We saw through the "peace speeches" of Hitler. We did not fall for his speeches. However, no matter how much we exiles attempted to preach to the world the dangers ahead, nobody wanted to listen. Hitler could have been contained in 1935, or maybe even in 1936. But he would never have given up even if rebuffed in his aims for the Rhineland or for Austria. He would never have renounced his final aim of European, or maybe world, conquest.

Even in that last stage in the bunker in Berlin, when everything was lost, Hitler still dreamt of a reversal of alliances when he heard about Roosevelt's death. He felt that the great turn had come and that Germany might still be victorious. He was a doctrinaire fanatic, completely obsessed with the idea of conquest and hegemony.

I do not believe that you can apply that kind of ideology to the Soviets from Stalin onwards. That is why I have tried in my presentation to contrast the early dreams of Lenin with the Soviet Union of Stalin and the post-Stalin era.

Lenin was interested in the spread of world revolution, in a genuine world revolutionary internationalism with the Soviet Union as its core. The Stalinist and post-Stalinist Soviet Union has certain objectives as a super-power. I do not see a basic difference between the objectives of the Soviet Union, let us say in the Near East or in the Far East or anywhere else, and those of the United States, namely, to vie for influence. Neither is interested in expanding territorially.

I may, however, be mistaken. There may be "ideological" opposition in the Politbureau which does not agree with the present Soviet leadership on this point. If so, I believe we can be glad to have Brezhnev at the helm. This may sound strange, but just imagine we were faced with an opponent of Brezhnev's detente policy, then we would see something. Then we would yearn for the times when one could still speak with "reasonable" people, relatively reasonable people, like Khrushchev or Brezhnev. Of course they had to be contained. But Americans too had to be contained. Otherwise we would rule the world today.

MIROSLAV TODOROVICH, *Bronx Community College*

I beg to differ with Professor Herz on several points. Zinoviev was wrong at the time on the actual timetable. However, presently there exist many more "revolutionary" communist governments, and they may even create some trouble for their mother country. The fact is that there has been an expansion of communist governments over the years.

It has been emphasized that we have a kind of stabilized situation in the Western world. I would point out that this stabilization is more the remnant of the past cold war attitudes of the two super powers than anything that would result from what happened later, the so-called spirit of detente. And those of us who are observing from various corners the present attempts by some of our leaders to develop what they call the new politics of detente, are precisely concerned with what will come next, rather than

what we have now! Between the two wars there were many
people in Europe, in coffee houses, in legislatures, and
elsewhere, who were making statements similar to those of
present day Meanys and others, and of course, they may
have been practicing people and not theoreticians as professors are. But many of the statements of these observers
proved to be more correct in 1938, 1939, and later, than
the pronouncements by "experts" who insisted that the
speeches by Hitler and others were mere rhetoric which
should not be taken seriously.

But I do not want in any way to prejudge the discussion.
I just think that those who are worried about their present
friends have the same right to put their money on the table
as are those who are or may be over optimistic.

KLAUS PRINGSHEIM, *McMaster University, Canada*

I am vaguely uncomfortable with Professor Herz' thesis
that Brezhnev is a reasonable man, and that he is more to
be trusted and less likely to dissimulate than others. I think
it is very easy to be a reasonable man when you have a
large person with a gun standing at your side. Mr. Brezhnev is very reasonable because he has eight hundred million Chinese looking over his shoulder. How reasonable is
Mr. Brezhnev going to be after the present Chinese government has been perhaps overthrown by one which is
more friendly to Mr. Brezhnev? I am not saying that this is
going to happen. But I am saying that it might happen. If it
happens, is he going to be reasonable? Is he going to see to
it that the Israelis are obliterated? Is he going to see to it
that Yugoslavia is occupied, that Rumania is occupied, and
that perhaps the Italian Communist party is brought to
power by other means than democratic parliamentary
means?

You see, I really do not believe in this reasonability of
Mr. Brezhnev. We have an interesting balance at the moment. Mr. Brezhnev is in very great danger. When he
looks over his shoulder he says, "Yes, yes, very nice, Mr.
Kissinger; come and have six hours of talks with me, par-

ticularly while I am deathly worried about what might happen with the Chinese." But when the situation changes, watch Mr. Brezhnev.

JOHN H. HERZ, *The City University of New York*

Reasonableness is a relative concept. You may be reasonable for very different reasons. Maybe I should not have used the term "reasonableness." But whether Brezhnev or whoever else is in power, or will be in power, in the Soviet Union or in Washington, for that matter, I would say that reasonableness is not only caused by that big man in the back, but also, and even more so, by the fact that if you fail to be reasonable, you or the other fellow may blow up the world. The nuclear factor is the primary one which instills reasonableness into leaders.

It is enough for me to know that there are certain factors in the situation which compel leaders to be reasonable unless they want to act like irrational Hitlers.

Q. ADOLFO COMBA, Director, *The New York Office of the Commission of the European Communities*

I am not speaking now in my official capacity, but as an Italian citizen. I just heard that the attempt by Mr. Fanfani to form a coalition government has failed. A decision has not been made on whether to have reelections or try to form a coalition government with the communists, or at least with their external support.

Now I would like to ask Professor Herz whether he is willing to risk his reputation on a corollary that I could draw from his theory that in fact deterrence is such that except for minor territorial adjustments, neither of the two super powers would be willing to change their fundamental postures on detente. I also draw the conclusion that it is a factor in detente on the side of the Soviet Union to try to preserve a certain balance in the West so as to be reciprocally left in charge of its own detente problems in the eastern part of Europe.

Would Professor Herz risk his reputation by accepting

the fact that there would not be any catastrophic consequences for the western world, as Dr. Kissinger seems to say and imply, if the Italian communist party went into the government?

A. JOHN H. HERZ, *The City University of New York*

I do not know enough about the Italian government really to venture an answer here. But it seems to me that the communist parties in western Europe, particularly the Italian and French parties, have become so *status quo* minded that taking these parties into a coalition government may, perhaps, be the best guarantee for preserving the present system in these countries. You know better than I do that the communists in Italy have already gained quite some influence in local and regional affairs, and they have proved to be, as the French party did in 1968, one of the stabilizing elements in the situation.

I would agree with what you seem to intimate, namely, that it is present Soviet policy not to disturb the present balance of power in Europe. The present balance would, of course, be disturbed if they were to find France and Italy belonging to the eastern bloc, or to go over to the eastern bloc. That is why I tried to point out that the Russians are not interested at the present time in even taking over, if they could, the western part of Germany.

FRANK D. GRANDE, *The City College of New York*

I disagree with the notion that bringing the communist party of Italy—or of any other country—into the cabinet might somehow help to preserve the current system. We have to distinguish between the short run tactics and the long range objectives of the communist parties. Certainly they have been able to attract the votes and membership of many people who are willing to operate within the framework of a democracy. But I think the communist parties, like the fascist parties, have a hard core determined ultimately to overturn the system by any means necessary. They may use the parliamentary process as a means for gaining power. But what will they do once they have fully secured that power in the national government, rather than just in local areas? It seems to me that a party so thoroughly imbued with a totalitarian ideology will not, in the long run, compromise. And to think we can make them change their ultimate goal is, in my opinion, a naive view of politics.

But in the sphere of international relations, I think the problem is quite different: even a country like Soviet Russia, founded on an anti-nationalist ideology, may become obliged to respect the idea of a balance of power —provided, of course, we unequivocally reassert our commitment to a policy of preserving the nation-state system and defending the balance of power in that sense on a permanent basis. This means we must cast off all ambiguities about our goals in foreign affairs. (We often comport ourselves like a sovereign nation, but sometimes our actions are contradicted by policy statements which tend toward some vague expression of the desire for a world community.)

Furthermore, I believe that a close analysis of Henry Kissinger's writings would indicate that our Secretary of State does not really believe in *Staatsraison*, as he sometimes would like us to think. Rather, he seems to have elevated to an absolute value some vague cosmopolitan ideal of world peace at a considerable expense of our national interests. I would maintain that such ideas are a needless provocation to our professed enemies and actually retard the working out of relations based on the full mutual respect due nations which occupy separate and equal stations. It is conceivable, of course, that the Russians may view such statements of a cosmopolitan ideal simply as part of an attempt to trick them. It is much more likely, however, that they are preparing for a final convergence similar to the confrontation that occurred between the Bolsheviks and Kerensky in Moscow in 1917.

JOHN H. HERZ, *The City University of New York*

In regard to Italy and the communist party, I would like to say two things. First it depends on whether the others would allow a communist party which enters a coalition —and certainly would not be the majority party or the majority group in that coalition—to prevail. In other words, there has to be internally also a policy of containment —and, of course, if the others behave stupidly and let the communists take over, that would be a different situation. Second, however, I come back to my hunch that, as I would put it, the present communist parties in western Europe can be compared with the SPD or other social democratic parties in the 20's—in other words, parties that are more or less resigned to play the game within the existing system and have given up world revolutionary ideology.

On the other comment, I would never have thought that I would sit here and come out as defender of Mr. Kissinger, but I must say that to characterize him as a utopian idealist does not quite agree with what I know of Henry Kissinger's writings and of his attitudes and policies. He is a detente man, yes, but certainly not one who is in favor of giving up American sovereignty—even a little bit of American sovereignty—if you take that in the sense of yielding something which would make us part of a super-government, a world government, or something like that.

Perhaps what you really meant to refer to is his recent conversion to committing the United States to closer and broader international cooperation in the great global crisis areas (such as population explosion, threatening exhaustion of vital resources, threat to the global environment, energy crisis, monetary crisis, etc.). If that makes him (or me, or anybody else) a "cosmopolitan idealist," make the most of it.

FRANK D. GRANDE, *The City College of New York*

It's not easy to pin down Henry Kissinger on the question of his ultimate goals. But I would maintain that, amid all the ambiguities and paradoxes in his writings and speeches, the goal of an enforceable world peace has become readily more discernible. In *The Necessity for Choice* Kissinger says that the West, which has given the concept of nationalism to the world, must now "show the way to a new international order." And he has come back to this theme again and again. I realize, of course, that the full implications of such statements may be subject to widely varying interpretations. But how can one account for the Secretary of State's speech to the United Nations last year? There he began by recalling Immanuel Kant's prediction that universal peace is inevitable, and then spoke of dedicating ourselves to "a world in which the rule of law governs" and a "comprehensive, institutionalized peace." If Professor Herz is correct, then we might be forced to conclude that Dr. Kissinger was being hypocritical on that occasion. But I prefer to take him seriously. And I must insist that such a goal requires us to ask some hard questions. Who will make the final decisions necessary for enforcing the world peace? Indeed, is it possible to establish an enforceable world peace without some universal peace keeping agency that would have an absolute monopoly of coercive power? And would that peace keeping agency be anything other than a universal tyranny of the strongest nation in the world? I fear the result would be similar to that which the historian Eduard Meyer saw as the inevitable result of ancient Rome's pacification of the entire Mediterranean world—men losing the sense of true freedom without which human life is hardly distinguishable from that of animals.

# PART II
# DETENTE SINCE 1945

# Policy Debate in the Kissinger Era

GIL CARL ALROY

In addressing great issues of foreign policy, this session and the conference fill a particularly important need at this time. For rarely in the past was there such a dearth of serious public discussion of foreign policy as now. Secretary Kissinger has made foreign policy utterly personal and secretive and himself both interpreter and arbiter of policy and the national interest. Far from fulfilling its task of independent reporting and investigation, the press of this country has been turned by the special circumstances of Watergate, inherent weaknesses, and extraordinary manipulation by Kissinger himself, into his compliant instrument. A former senior staff member of the National Security Council under Kissinger, who detailed the corruption of the press, indicated that, as a result, the public may not even be aware of the issues to be probed, much less the need to probe at all.[1] The media serve to inform the country to a great extent in accordance with his perceptions, yardsticks, and desires. Obvious failures loom as puzzles, while any success comes across as epochal. How can there be serious public debate under these circumstances?

As folk hero, Secretary Kissinger acquires a certain immunity also from interference by other government officials, particularly from the Congress, which is torn between the duty to check and probe and the imperative of heeding the people's adulation of the Secretary. The alacrity with which the otherwise formidable Senate decided to forego inquiring into his involvement in Watergate lest he leave illustrates this unusual situation.

Not only is there extraordinary trusting reliance on the Secretary, indeed virtual immunity from the press and the politicians, but the very exaltation discourages professional analysts of international affairs as well. They not only find it difficult to reach the broader public, but feel that the attempt itself may be unpleasant. "Up against hero worship," another former Kissinger aide has written, "legitimate criticism begins to sound like ungrateful grousing."[2]

The Secretary himself does nothing to encourage debate of policy. His characteristic response to query or criticism, when it occurs, is a power confrontation or public relations maneuver. The exposure of his role in Chile and his deception of the Congress in this matter was not addressed; instead, the President appeared to exculpate his Secretary and put an end to questions. The policy on Cyprus appeared to stir much national unhappiness, and was not addressed either. Instead, there followed a publicity stroke in the form of an interview with James Reston, featured as a grand public event, in which a friendly journalist allows the Secretary to skirt the real issues, taking instead a pose as philosopher of history assaying his place in the records of humankind.[3] Kissinger's "explanation" of his conduct in the October War in the Middle East is to nurture a book by other such conduits, featuring a fairy-tale version of the events.[4] The man who doggedly "tilted" against Israel throughout the war comes across in this best-seller as desperately struggling for her.[5]

Thomas L. Hughes has recently warned that the cost of Kissinger's personalism may be disastrous for the United

States. "Personalism," he wrote, "often tends to prefer the superficial and the transitory over the deep and fundamental. Personalism has a short-term time-table. It is tempted to take benefits now and leave the unknown costs to its successors. The more intractable the problem and far-reaching the measures required to meet it, the more a narrow leadership will be tempted to indulge in pseudo-solutions· for appearances' sake. Personalism tends to deal with the thin crust of affairs, to concentrate on personal arrangements for the moment rather than partnership arrangements for the future. . . . Faced with unfulfillable requirements, personalism naturally prefers the episodic over the continuing, the specialized over the comprehensive, the spasmodic over the consistent, the urgent over the pervasive."[6]

His suggestion that, as the euphoria diminishes, we will begin to distinguish between our foreign policy as it has recently been perceived and our foreign policy as it has actually been pursued, has already been supported by what little probing has been done into Kissinger's policy. Thus Tad Szulc's study of the Vietnam cease-fire negotiations has revealed a reality so disparate in some respect with the conventional wisdom as to be shocking to the few who read it.[7] My own study of Kissinger's involvement in Middle East affairs indicates that his celebrated successes rest on dubious real accomplishments, other than manipulation for immediate and personal advantage, and may well have gravely set back lasting American interests and the chances of real peace in that part of the world.[8] Even though we already know more than enough for the kind of open and public discussion needed to take stock of our condition and direction at so critical a time for ourselves and the whole West and masses of humanity outside of it, such discussion started to take shape so far only in respect to the issues before us here today.

It is detente, where at least some substantial critique has both been voiced and aired to broader audiences. This is attributable in part to the popular appeal of the struggle of Soviet Jewry and the civil rights movement, with Solzhenitsyn and other international heroes. Having been frustrated in the Congress, the Secretary himself recently called for a national debate on detente. But it appears that he has not yet relented from a stance that confuses the issues and demeans the discussants. For surely the real question is not whether one is against nuclear holocaust and for better relations with the other superpower, as he has repeatedly insinuated. The real issues start with the very concept of detente, its function, its uses and disuses for the national interest and international aspirations. The stakes are immense and we have barely begun.

## NOTES

1. Roger Morris, "Henry Kissinger and the Media: A Separate Peace," *Columbia Journalism Review*, Vol. 13, No. 1, May-June, 1974.

2. Anthony Lake, "An End to Either/Or," *The New York Times*, August 12, 1974, p. 23.

3. *The New York Times*, October 13, 1974.

4. See Ronald Steel's review of the book, *Kissinger*, by Marvin Kalb and Bernard Kalb, in *The New York Times Review of Books*, Vol. 21, No. 14, September 19, 1974.

5. See Edward Luttwak and Walter Laqueur, "Kissinger and the Yom Kippur War," *Commentary*, Vol. 58, No. 3, September, 1974.

6. "Foreign Policy: Men or Measures?" *The Atlantic*, Vol. 234, No. 4, October, 1974, pp. 59-60.

7. "Behind the Vietnam Cease-Fire Agreement," *Foreign Policy*, No. 15, Summer, 1974.

8. *The Kissinger Experience* (New York: Horizon Press, 1975).

# Detente:
# Reality and Illusion

## HANS J. MORGENTHAU

The Secretary of State has asked for a national debate on the policy of detente. But the problem has been posed in terms which are simply not susceptible to rational debate. I am referring here to the very concept we are dealing with. Detente is one of those concepts which have a positive moral connotation. Obviously you cannot be against detente and in favor of bigger and better tensions. It is the same type of concept—it belongs to the same class of concepts —as peace, general and complete disarmament, security, relaxation of tensions, peaceful coexistence. All these concepts have two things in common. They disarm critical analysis for the reason I have just mentioned. But behind those concepts the ordinary business, the traditional business, of foreign policy goes on, thinly disguised by those concepts.

The real political question is not what detente means in the dictionary sense but what political purposes it serves. What are the political policies on behalf of which the term "detente" is invoked? When you probe behind a term such as detente you realize that it is a typical ideology of foreign policy. That is to say, it is not a foreign policy by itself, but it is an attempt to justify on rational and moral grounds whatever policy is being pursued and to invoke rational and moral arguments on behalf of whatever policy the term detente is invoked. It is characteristic of the popular approach to foreign policy in this country that those general concepts, those abstractions with a positive moral connotation have an enormous impact upon public opinion. For they in a sense anticipate the expected and wished-for results of the particular foreign policy. Obviously it would be a great world if peace would reign unchallenged, if all nations would abolish their armed forces, if tension were relaxed, if all nations would enjoy security and coexist peacefully with each other, and if there were detente between nations which formerly were on opposite sides of the fence. So the invocation of detente has a deleterious effect upon rational understanding of foreign policy and rational discourse on the contended issues of foreign policy.

To do justice to the claim that detente has occurred between the United States and the Soviet Union one has to lower one's sight from those abstractions and look at the actual situation throughout the world. In other words, one has to ask oneself: where have tensions existed in the past which have pitted the United States against the Soviet Union and where have those tensions been abated or eliminated? One has to proceed as do the French and British Foreign Ministers at the beginning of the parliamentary session. They make a *tour d'horizon;* they go step by step from one country to the other and explain in what ways the national interests have been affected by the foreign policy of the particular country and by world events. If we do this, if we ask ourselves where tensions between the United States and the Soviet Union have actually been abated or eliminated, we arrive at a rational result which shows that in two fields there has been real detente and in others there has been no detente at all. We can even go so far as to say that with regard to those issues where there has not been any detente at all, the very invocation of detente, the holding of the American government to the ideal of detente, to the alleged reality of detente, has done more harm than good to the interests of the United States and of the world.

It is obvious that in one very important area there has been genuine detente, and that is the area of ideological confrontation between the United States and the Soviet Union or, if I may use terms which had currency during the cold war period, between the free world and communism. It is interesting that when one uses today such terms as "free world versus communism" one has to make a kind of mental reservation because this juxtaposition of two terms goes back to the period of the cold war and to the period of the ideological confrontation between the United States and the Soviet Union. You have a very clear indication of the radical change which has occurred in this respect when you compare, let me say, the pronouncements of Eisenhower and Dulles with the public statements of Nixon, Ford, and Kissinger, more particularly the annual reports of the President on the state of the world. Those reports, which are in part quite intelligent and penetrating (showing who has written what in the report), are virtually free of ideological argumentation. The word "communist" hardly appears in them. Compare this kind of ideological decontamination with the rhetoric of Eisenhower and Dulles, which was full of arguments against "godless communism" and in favor of "liberation" and "roll-back" and in which the history of the world was shown as an inevitable confrontation between good and evil, freedom and communism, and there was never any doubt who would of necessity win. All this has disappeared.

You may say this is a rhetorical change which did not affect the substance of foreign policy itself, and to a certain extent you are right. For this ideological decontamination goes hand in hand with the anti-communist policy which the same team of Nixon and Kissinger pursued in Chile and Greece and which Ford and Kissinger continue to pursue in Indochina. Thus on the level of concrete policies we still cling to this conception that there is a conflict going on not only between two great powers, the United States and the Soviet Union, but between two philosophies, ways of life, moral orders, and foreign policy serves the purpose to defend one against encroachment by the other. But this is not to say that the change in rhetoric, the absence of this ideological fanaticism, is not a positive achievement, for it

makes civilized intercourse between the leaders of the two
superpowers possible in the first place. Certainly the kind
of social amenities which the respective statesmen receive
in different capitals are not mere social phenomena, but
have a distinctively political connotation. For it is possible
to argue on concrete issues, to negotiate, to bargain, to deal
with each other through the give-and-take of compromise
only after the conflicts have been divested of their ideological nature and have been reduced to manageable, pragmatic
proportions which can be dealt with by competent statesmen. The very fact that the United States and the Soviet
Union can negotiate about a settlement in the Middle East,
nuclear arms control, and other issues is in good measure
due to this ideological decontamination, which is a real,
genuine result of detente.

The second area in which detente has obviously had a
positive effect, that is, has actually occurred, is not due
primarily to the policies of the United States but to the
policies of the government of the Federal Republic of Germany under former Chancellor Brandt. The territorial focus
of the conflict between the United States and the Soviet
Union since the end of World War II has been the territorial settlement in Central Europe. It was, in other words,
the crucial question to which side Germany would belong,
to the East or to the West, which created the cold war,
and it was the refusal of a succession of governments of the
Federal Republic of Germany to recognize the territorial
status quo which had been established by virtue of the distribution of military forces at the end of World War II
which sustained the cold war. You have only to remember
that a few years ago the formerly German provinces which
are now administered as integral parts of Poland and the
Soviet Union were officially called "East Germany" by the
West German government. What we call here East Germany was called "Middle Germany" or the "Soviet zone of
occupation," and the only legitimate German government

was supposed to be the government of Bonn. The Hallstein doctrine in addition stipulated the refusal of the West German government to have diplomatic relations with any country which recognized the East German government. So you had a situation which was politically unmanageable since nothing could be done about it short of a victorious war, but which was declared illegitimate by the United States and the West German government. And the Soviet Union responded to this refusal to recognize the legitimacy of the territorial status quo by continuing violent polemics against a succession of governments of the Federal Republic.

All this real tension in the classic sense over a piece of territory which both sides claim has virtually disappeared; it has virtually been eliminated by the *Ostpolitik* of former Chancellor Brandt. There remains the existential issue of West Berlin about which nobody can do anything because West Berlin, for better or for worse, is located within the territory of the Eastern bloc. Aside from this issue, which can be resuscitated in the form of tension any time the East German or the Soviet government wants to resuscitate it, the issue of the territorial status quo in Central Europe has been settled. This is indeed an enormous achievement if you compare it with the festering wound which poisoned East-West relations for twenty-five years after the end of World War II. Here real detente has taken place. But I would emphasize again that it has not been detente by virtue of American policy. Our government was rather reluctant to support Mr. Brandt's *Ostpolitik* and was quite uneasy about the possible consequences. But, as a matter of fact, here real detente has occurred.

If you look at the rest of the world, at the points of conflict which have existed or have emerged between the United States and the Soviet Union since the end of World War II, there has been no detente. The same tensions exist as existed before because the same incompatible objectives exist on both sides of the dividing line. And here is the intellectual and political danger in the use of the term "detente." We assume that there is a policy of detente, that is to say, a policy which is inspired by detente, where detente, in other words, reveals itself in the actual actions taken by governments, rather than detente being the result of a particular policy. Detente, ill-used in this sense, becomes a disarming factor in the policies of nations which fall under the spell of this word and take it as a reflection of reality rather than as an aim of a policy to be realized in the future. Take for instance the Middle East.

The Middle Eastern policy of the United States since the October War of 1973 has been clearly inspired by one basic objective: at least to limit, if not to eliminate, Soviet influence in the Middle East. The issue is not whether this country should have that territory or that country should have another piece of territory. The issue is simply to pursue a policy which promises to take the wind out of the sails of the Soviet Union. When the October War broke out, the United States appealed to the Soviet Union to approach the conflict "in the spirit of detente." What did the Soviet Union do? After having armed the Arab countries and after having been informed of the impending outbreak of the war, if not having planned it, it urged all the Arab governments which had not initially participated in the war to do so. When Syria and Egypt were at the verge of defeat, the Soviet Union urged the United States to join it in sending troops to the Middle East to enforce a ceasefire, warning the United States that if it did not do so, the Soviet Union would do it unilaterally, at the same time mobilizing some of its parachute troops. Whereupon the United States mobilized its strategic forces and threatened to send troops to Sinai if the Soviet Union sent troops to Egypt. Furthermore, we learned from our intelligence that the Soviet Union was sending a ship loaded with nuclear warheads to the port of Alexandria. In other words, we were thus involved in the kind of confrontation which had been classically established at the beginning of the Cuban missile crisis of 1962. There was a threat of military intervention, a counterthreat of military action, and a retreat from those exposed positions on both sides because of the risk of nuclear war. In consequence, no troops were sent to the Middle East by either side. The Russian ship turned around and went back to where it came from, and peace was preserved.

But detente had absolutely nothing to do with this situation. It was a classic example of a political-military situation which has occurred in the world many times before and in the relations between the United States and the Soviet Union once with classic clarity during the Cuban missile crisis. However, I want to call your attention again to the intellectual and political damage which the illusion of detente may create in the minds of those who believe in it as the substance of policy rather than the end result of policy. The idea that the Soviet Union would all of a sudden forget about power politics when it was confronted with the issues of the Middle East, that it would allow itself to be pushed out of the Middle East in the spirit of detente, was of course an absolute illusion. So it was, you may say, the common sense of our administration which won the day over an ephemeral hope that the Russians would be nice, would forget about their objectives and the means they had at their disposal to support those objectives, and act "in the spirit of detente."

Thus it is here that the real problematic of detente arises. It creates public expectations which may or may not be fulfilled, and it leads to a fundamental misunderstanding of the relationship between means and ends in foreign policy. For it takes the end result of a political action, of a political policy, as being inherent in the policy itself. So it is not surprising that detente has not created the kind of meaningful public debate which the Secretary of State invited us to begin. The term does not lend itself to such a debate. It does not deal with foreign policy as such.

It deals with the possible, and you may say desirable, results of such a policy. For detente in this sense is really no different from peace or security or peaceful coexistence or the relaxation of tensions, or all the other similarly abstract concepts which the Soviet Union has floated in order to muddle our thinking and to gain the reputation of moral superiority over the United States. The Soviet Union has always posed as the defender of those concepts, which it launched in the first place, while under the cover of those rhetorical pronouncements it has pursued the age-old policies of Russia which, in the Middle East as elsewhere, have a very respectable ancestry under the aegis of Czarism. What we call today the Middle Eastern question, one hundred years ago was called the Eastern Question, and instead of the United States being pitted against the Soviet Union, Great Britain was pitted against Russia. For there are certain geo-political facts which are immutable, as immutable as geography itself, and the fact that the Middle East is a land bridge joining three continents is one of those facts.

To this fact is added today the political use of oil, an unprecedented event in political history. For all of a sudden, countries which can hardly be called nations in any meaningful sense, which have absolutely no power of any kind, have become enormously powerful, in a sense have acquired the power over life and death of nations without oil, because they possess a quasi-monopoly of what has become the lifeblood of modern industrial and technological societies.

While no two events in history are exactly identical and, hence, there are no exact analogies, the core of the problem which we are facing in the Middle East and which has pitted us against the Soviet Union is the same power- and geo-political problem which Great Britain faced one hundred years ago. So if one wants to have a meaningful public debate on American foreign policy and, more particularly, the new American foreign policy which Nixon and

Kissinger have initiated and which, in my view, has much to be said in favor of it, one has to get away from those meaningless abstractions which, far from guiding us to an understanding of foreign policy, really inhibit that understanding. It can be said that this misdirection of our attention has become one of the secret, or perhaps not so secret, weapons with which the Soviet Union has opposed our interests and has tried to paralyze our will and our understanding of our interests as well as the interests of the world, and of the policies best suited to support those interests.

# *Ostpolitik*: Detente from a European Perspective

PETER C. LUDZ

Detente, like other foreign policy devices, is part of international politics and subject to continuous changes. Our present views on West-East relations and, thus, our understanding of detente are quite different from the ones held four, or even two years ago. A number of events have required changes in detente strategy and, consequently, in our thinking about its implications.

Despite the strong and substantial pessimism of many Western observers of the international scene, the policy of detente was able to regain a footing even after the Arab-Israeli crisis in 1973. Although the early dynamic of detente was lost, the policy itself was not abandoned. In modified form, US-Soviet detente still constitutes an essential feature of the structure of peace, and the reason is obvious: for both nations detente is, as Zbigniew Brzezinski put it, a "welcome development, for its absence would imply a continuing arms race, conducted in an atmosphere of hostility and tension."[1] This conclusion corresponds with views held by other analysts. Hans Morgenthau, for instance, made it clear that "peace between the two superpowers has been preserved not through detente but through the nuclear balance of terror. . . . Thus it is not detente that makes for peace, but it is the nuclear balance that makes both for detente and peace."[2]

Although we still seem to live in an era of detente, the tendencies toward an easing of the strained West-East relationship have slackened considerably. This situation is creating efforts toward a more differentiated understanding of the meaning of detente, of its possibilities and limitations.

In the United States and elsewhere in the West, one has begun to realize that the cold war period will not be followed by an era of friendship between the East and the West, nor even a rapprochement in basic principles and norms. On the other hand, one is well aware that the nuclear balance and detente are not operating "mechanically." Rather, they require "a consensus among the nations involved in favor of the maintenance—or, if it should be disturbed, of the restoration—of the balance of power. In other words, the dynamics of the arrangement are embedded in a moral framework without which, in the long run, it cannot operate."[3]

These new insights entail a reconsideration of the meaning of detente, which may be facilitated by an examination of the changes that have occurred in the conception of detente in *Ostpolitik*. Contrary to the times of Willy Brandt's and Egon Bahr's *Ostpolitik*, alteration of the status quo has been achieved and is no longer a priority. The problem of detente now is to maintain the status quo. Today, in contrast to several years ago, detente is less a political conception that impels us to seek new improvements in West-East relations. It no longer points to a strategy of building new bridges to the East. It no longer fits into the model of an active and dynamic Western policy of coexistence and cooperation, as was described by Marshall Shulman in late 1973.[4] It has become a strategy used more to limit conflicts and to reduce the possibility of conflicts. Its emphasis now is to preserve the existing and rather fragile balance of forces in world politics.

For Western foreign policies this new state of affairs requires different political styles and orientations, such as vigilance, caution, shrewd and hard bargaining, and sharp awareness of the effects of detente on the independent actions of countries whose policies are now being formulated unilaterally—i.e. especially, the Arab States.

In Europe these changes in international politics call for an additional re-orientation. The wish to establish a political community comparable to those of the two superpowers, i.e., to become a third or fourth major power in world politics—as expressed in 1973 by Michel Jobert, then the French Secretary of State, and Egon Bahr, then a minister-without-portfolio in the West German government—must now be modified to fit the new situation. Although a united Europe remains the goal to be worked for, the aspiration of becoming a superpower can no longer express the major line of European politics. Rather, the Europeans must acknowledge that the new circumstances and the requirements of military and economic security reassert the strong necessity for Western Europe to lean upon the United States.

II.

Focussing on the years 1969 thru 1973—the years when German policy toward its Eastern neighbors was made by Willy Brandt, Walter Scheel and Egon Bahr—one may readily see that *Ostpolitik* was not only an integral part of the global policy of US-USSR detente, but also contributed to a stabilization of the European political situation by abandoning that policy which insisted on having the German question resolved as a whole and only within the context of a peace treaty. The Federal Republic of Germany (FRG) had always been a strong supporter of moves toward West European political and economic integration and adherence to the Atlantic alliance with the United States. This policy was continued during the years 1969-1973, and has since been continued even though *Ostpolitik* was thrust into the background when Helmut Schmidt became chancellor. The key point is that West Germany's *Ostpolitik* has always been inseparable from its *Westpolitik*. Thus its *Ostpolitik* did not weaken its *Westpolitik*, but probably strengthened it because more than any other West European state the FRG has been and remains committed to the idea of a united Europe. In part, this is due to the Federal

Republic's lack of a national consciousness, which *Ostpolitik* brought into a clear perspective.

Thus *Ostpolitik*, which in the beginning was viewed with suspicion by some of Bonn's most important allies, soon became an established part of international affairs. The United States and West Germany's European allies came to recognize that *Ostpolitik* was in fact the other side of *Westpolitik* because the initiatives of the Federal Republic in foreign affairs have endangered neither the Atlantic alliance nor the integration of the FRG into the European Community. On the contrary, the Federal Republic's ties with the West have become stronger. This can be gathered from the fact that on every possible occasion—for example, at the European summit meeting in the autumn of 1972—the FRG has submitted realistic proposals for a further unification of Europe. Moreover, the achievements of *Ostpolitik* have complemented the United States' own policy of detente. Efforts toward a mutual renunciation of the use of force—the most important principle in the 1970 treaty between the Federal Republic and the Soviet Union as well as in the 1972 treaty between the Federal Republic and the German Democratic Republic (GDR)—form part of the basis of American-Soviet relations. Thus the policies of the FRG toward its East European neighbors, which earlier in detente appeared to be running contrary to the interests of the United States, have in fact been running in tandem.

Without doubt, the aspect of *Ostpolitik* that received most attention abroad was the Basic Treaty *(Grundlagenvertrag)* between the FRG and the GDR, which became effective in 1973. In this agreement, the FRG formally recognized the status quo of a divided Germany. However, the treaty did not impair the concept of common interests and traditions in both parts of Germany or the principle of self-determination for the German nation as a whole. Differences of opinion on questions such as German unity were bridged by way of a statement agreeing to disagree. The disputes were settled before the two German states entered the United Nations with the intention of entertaining the world with as few *querelles allemandes* as possible. Above all, the pact between the two German states showed that the willingness to alter inner-German relations did not endanger political stability because it was based on a mutual renunciation of force. Indeed, the section in the treaty confirming the inviolability of existing borders is an essential element of the agreement. By including the GDR in its *Ostpolitik*, and thereby recognizing the East Berlin government as an equal partner in European affairs, the FRG made another decisive contribution to political stability and normalization in Europe. In this context it is also necessary to point out that *Ostpolitik*, as part of a far-reaching European peace policy, set the pace for political multilateralism on the continent. Here again what appeared to be an independent course of action (that might violate existing commitments to NATO and the European Community) can be seen as having set what is now the pattern for Europe's nations in their relations with each other and with the United States.

Without the achievements of *Ostpolitik*, neither the preparatory meeting, held at Helsinki in the summer of 1973, nor the constitutive meeting of the Conference for Security and Cooperation in Europe (CSCE), still in progress in Geneva, would have been possible. The goal of creating a system for a viable peace in Europe meant acceptance of detente and political normalization. It meant that these issues took precedence over German reunification (which few outside of Germany really wanted anyway). It meant accepting existing realities in Germany and bidding farewell to Bismarck's Empire. It meant a recognition of interdependence in the world through a system of treaties. It meant all this and more: acceptance of the largest possible spectrum for transnational cooperation; for competitive cooperation, rather than an *a priori* insistence on selective cooperation. For the FRG this also meant taking into consideration the changing role of the Soviet Union, the German Democratic Republic, and the other nations of Eastern Europe. The opponent had not ceased to be the opponent, but had become in addition a rival and a competitor (primarily in socio-economic matters). Instead of defence and counter defense, the most important question had become: which form of mass industrial society would be the wave of the future.

The political significance of the *Ostpolitik* for the Atlantic alliance as well as for the integration of Western Europe thus had three major aspects: (1) it set a trend for furthering detente in Europe; (2) it strengthened the Western alliance; and (3) it convincingly demonstrated the value of interdependence and self-imposed limitations in an era of "security through agreement."

For the first time West Germany had been able to transcend the parochialism of its view of the German question and actively to participate in international affairs. In this respect the ending of the cold war also meant the beginning of a new chapter in the Federal Republic's political history.

### III.

Any consideration of *Ostpolitik* must recognize its inherent ambivalence. From the start, it coincided with a rapidly changing international political situation, a set disparity in the armament race, and an increasing disposition for East-West cooperation. There was a desire for more security, stronger integration in the West, and recognition of the status quo; likewise, there was a greater chance for a mutual renunciation of the use of force, all-European cooperation, and a transformation of the status quo. There was also a desire for a reduction of the conflicts, for written agreements and a willingness to accept new principles of political behavior. At the same time, there were still the ever-present risks that a latent conflict might emerge or that standing agreements might be jeopardized by a new interpretation. An avoidance of new conflicts was accom-

panied by an increased awareness of existing conflicts and
their potential expansion. Despite being conceived on a
solid basis of security, *Ostpolitik* contained countless risks.
Taking risks, however, does not mean one is irresponsible
or blind to existing realities. It can result in breakthroughs
to political innovations that, in the case of *Ostpolitik*, were
of advantage to both the West and the East.

The ambivalence of *Ostpolitik* had both positive and
negative aspects. On the positive side were a furthering of
detente and a relieving of confrontations, not to mention a
broadening of the political scope of the FRG. On the negative side was the fact that detente had to be understood as
a surmounting of the status quo. It is in this respect that
the detente policy of the FRG was distinguishable from the
detente policies of its Western allies. It was thought by
some in Britain, France, and elsewhere that the Basic Treaty between the two Germanies, which appeared to seal the
division of Germany, may in the long run paradoxically
weaken or overcome the division of Germany and of
Europe. There were some fears that the ambivalent character of *Ostpolitik* would delay *ad infinitum* a final decision
over the FRG's participation in Western European integration. Thus far these fears, as we all know, have not
materialized, and they seem not likely to do so in the near
future. This is especially true for the administration under
Chancellor Helmut Schmidt, for whom the economic and
the political unity of Western Europe has first priority.

It should be emphasized that the ambivalence in
*Ostpolitik* was in the interests of the West. In a certain
sense it was tailored to meet the intentions of what has
been called the Nixon-Kissinger doctrine. The combination
of loyalty to the allied partners, on the one hand, and
agreement to cooperate as well as to limit relations with a
political opponent, on the other (which presupposes the existence of alliances on both sides as well as leading them
into a new system of political principles and agreements),
was firmly anchored in German as well as in American

strategy. In both, one finds the concept of competitive cooperation with its wide possibilities, its exchange of signals of intended behavior, and its broad spectrum of tactical maneuvers. Therefore, there could hardly have been basic misunderstandings between the United States and the Federal Republic in the area of political philosophy and political strategy.

The ambivalence of *Ostpolitik* also worked to the particular advantage of the FRG because it helped to gain a strong negotiating position in relation to the West. The West German state became more credible to its immediate neighbors because it took the initiative in facing up to political realities in Europe. At present German reunification is a dead issue. Even as a long-range target, it can only have meaning within the framework of a European peace system.

With regard to the East, *Ostpolitik* presented a counter strategy to the policy of peaceful coexistence of the Soviet Union and its partners in Eastern Europe. The tension of ideological aggressiveness which extends to socio-political rivalry, the combination of offers of cooperation and a clearly delineated class struggle are all contained in *Ostpolitik*. Moreover, *Ostpolitik* also presented the Soviet Union and its East European allies with an ideological and socio-political challenge. This became all the more obvious when the Social Democratic Party of Germany (SPD) instituted a viable program for a democratic welfare state in the FRG.

In this connection one must keep in mind that the Soviet Union and the German Democratic Republic have had as strategic foreign policy goals the obtaining of the most favorable conditions for constructing and consolidating "socialism-communism." These favorable conditions included the consolidation of internal political and socio-economic affairs in the Eastern bloc countries, which, after all, meant political stabilization of the "international socialist system." In the early years of *Ostpolitik*, as well as now, peace and detente are regarded as necessary for survival, not only by the West but also by the East. As a result, it has become easier to calculate the methods and manner of the political *reservatio mentalis* of the Soviet Union. Thus, shared knowledge of the motives of the other increases certainty for everyone.

## IV.

There is yet another aspect to be considered in the assessment of the political advantages and disadvantages of *Ostpolitik*. Willy Brandt, who was the West German Chancellor from 1969 through 1974, was a charismatic leader. His charisma—by replacing to some extent ideological stability, which after all was one of the benefits of the cold war—facilitated the transition from the period of the cold war to the detente period. As Arthur Vidich has noted, "many governments which were legitimated by their pursuit of cold war politics came under pressure to find alternative legitimating ideologies." He based this statement on the following argument: Political legitimacy has been one of the common problems of modern industrial societies and their governing bureaucracies. Capitalist societies in particular—capitalism seen here as a specific system of business, bureaucracy, and industry—lack the dramatic elements necessary to create an appealing ideology of legitimation. It is only today that we have become aware that the cold war, in spite of being a period of enormous escalation of the potential for destruction, was a period of nuclear peace. At the same time the cold war provided a pattern for control of conflicts within and between countries.[5]

Willy Brandt, like other Western leaders, had to cope with this major problem of detente, i.e., the lack of a legitimating ideology. He attempted to mobilize what he called the "social energies" of Western Europe and thus to construct a new base for the political legitimation of the FRG. He attempted to combine the social energies of Europe with democratic socialism, which then would be appealing to new social groups and could play an integrative role. Of course, Brandt knew that democratic socialism could only be verified through the implementation of concrete social reforms. Consequently, problems in the fields of regional and city planning, property and rent reforms, and environmental programs were given as much priority as the fields of education and training. Also on the agenda were questions concerning a European wage policy, assimilation of varying models for workers' participation in management, as well as proposals to place big national firms and international corporations under feasible European controls.

This political program—however one may evaluate it—at that time attracted many groups: the members of the trade unions, the intellectuals, the youth.

It would be wrong to state that this policy failed. Rather it was pushed aside by the issues raised by the world-wide economic crisis, which in many respects has now become a source of legitimation for many governments—i.e., external threats to internal peace and economic stability may be used to forge a unification of public opinion. This point is all the more important for West Germany because there is no longer the "embarrassment" of dependency on the United States.

V.

For the present, under Helmut Schmidt's chancellorship, West German foreign policy regarding the East and global detente may be described as follows:

1. Now, as before, West Germany's own interests are linked with the idea of global detente.

2. Now, as before, the FRG seeks to establish and develop relationships of peaceful coexistence and cooperation with its Eastern Warsaw Pact neighbors. Bonn seems to be well aware of the international significance of detente. Negotiations on strategic arms, the European Security Con-

ference and the question of force levels in Europe must be pursued, and the attempt to progress toward a peace settlement in the Middle East must command special and unremitting attention.

3. The Bonn government is also prepared to meet the international responsibilities which—as a side effect —Ostpolitik has burdened it with. However, one may question to what extent the FRG should become involved in some areas of USA-USSR competition. Such a question arises from a recent statement by Senator Edward Kennedy, who asked for greater European (and thus, West German) involvement in "some areas of US-Soviet competition, like the Middle East."[6] In this context mention should also be made of the fact that West Germany's present will to meet its international commitments is to some extent bound to the military presence of the United States in Europe and especially in Germany. Thus it is of major concern to all those familiar with German politics that US troops not be reduced considerably.

4. More than Willy Brandt, Helmut Schmidt may concentrate the energies of his administration on the political integration of Western Europe. He knows that in this Germany must play a key role. However, he may not wholeheartedly embark upon this path since, as much as anyone else, he realizes that progress in efforts toward European unification might result in hastening US withdrawal from the continent.

5. Ostpolitik, as was pointed out above, is no longer in the forefront of West German politics; but it is being continued by the Schmidt government. With regard to interGerman relations, for example, various issues of common interest are still being negotiated. At the top level, the FRG Undersecretary of State Gaus and GDR Deputy Minister of Foreign Affairs Nier are meeting regularly for discussions on future relations between the two German states. Also, the Basic Treaty has prepared the ground for detailed agreements between the FRG and the GDR on

postal and telephone matters, medical care, working conditions of journalists, and an agreement on sports, concluded on May 8, 1974. A contract on monetary matters is being prepared, and questions arising within the realm of the transit traffic between the FRG and West Berlin are being regularly brought up in a Standing Commission of FRG and GDR representatives. Moreover, the Basic Treaty required the institution of an official commission to settle border questions. By now, this commission may have marked about 20 per cent of the border that separates the two German states from each other. Exchange in judicial matters is another problem to be negotiated. Further, agreements on scientific and technological exchange programs, as well as on cultural matters, are in preparation. Both these latter agreements are, of course, highly dependent on the outcome of the CSCE negotiations in Geneva. Contacts between East and West Germany are also supposed to include environmental issues. These, however, are substantially affected by the erection of the Federal Agency for Environmental Affairs *(Umweltbundesamt)* in West Berlin, a step by the FRG government which the GDR and the Soviet Union have criticized vehemently.

From these agreements and negotiations—to say nothing of the many contacts between West Germany and other East European countries—it should be clear that *Ostpolitik* is still alive, and that many problems remain to be solved. Although some of the remaining problems may have to be redefined and placed into the new context of international detente policy, none of them threatens detente.

## VI.

There are now, however, entirely new issues that the West German government must tackle: the international economic difficulties; the new domesticism; and the ideological warfare in Europe, especially within Germany. Taking these issues into consideration, one is struck by the vulnerability of the policy of detente and wonders whether it will be able to deal with these new problems without actually transforming detente into something entirely different—even if it continues to be called by that name.

The international economic crisis has provided the most vivid examples of the vulnerability of detente. Not only did it produce tensions between Western Europe and the United States, but at certain points it also caused some West European countries to pursue their own individual interests vis-à-vis some Arab states, the Soviet Union, and other East European countries independently. This neglect of collective Western interests shook the ground on which Western detente policy was built.

The "new domesticism"—an expression coined by Pierre Hassner[7]—is an equal danger to detente. However, the shift of priorities to domestic issues in the FRG may also produce another effect. One of the strong beliefs held by the present West German Chancellor (as well as by the state secretaries for economic and financial affairs) is that at least some domestic issues, such as inflation and unemployment, cannot be dealt with unless West German political actions are coordinated with those of other European countries. The new domesticism may thus be viewed as resulting in new efforts toward multilateralization as well.

A third phenomenon that could weaken detente policy is the ideological war in Europe. The struggle on the ideological front between the East and the West has not halted in the aftermath of *Ostpolitik* and detente. This has been nowhere more evident than in the FRG in recent years.

It seems most important that the Western allies support the FRG in its ideological fight against the GDR and the Soviet Union. Undoubtedly the American policy of detente produced good results in so far as it made the ideological confrontation between Communism and the Free World disappear from the headlines of US and USSR newspapers. This development, however, did not affect other countries; and even in the USA and the USSR its scope was limited to official and officious declarations. We cannot, therefore, drop the ideological issues in order to do business with the Soviet Union and its East European partners. Rather, we should be aware of the fact that to refrain from openly and actively fighting for the democratic order on the ideological front can as much affect our security as any kind of military imbalance.

## VII.

Considering the achievements and present state of *Ostpolitik* within the context of the current detente debate, one may draw the following conclusions:

1. In 1969 *Ostpolitik* was long overdue. This explains the euphoric political outlook it helped to create.

2. *Ostpolitik* in its early phase marked the most spectacular stage in the policy of detente. And if there was ever a lack of realism in that policy, *Ostpolitik* most likely contributed to it.

3. Nevertheless, *Ostpolitik* as a political concept was rather successful. The list of its achievements is impressive: a relaxation of tensions in Europe; some concessions on the part of the Soviet Union with regard to both West German access to Berlin and all-German contacts; the inclusion of the FRG in international moves toward detente (in other words, the FRG's success in overcoming its isolation from the mainstreams of international politics); and finally the role *Ostpolitik* played in preparing the CSCE and in furthering political normalization in Europe.

4. West German officials, working under the umbrella of *Ostpolitik*, were among the first to encounter the toughness of their opponent negotiators, e.g., representatives from Czechoslovakia and East Germany.

5. Today *Ostpolitik* has become part of normal politics, due both to its own dynamic and the dynamic of international relations. Following political events in 1973 and 1974, the West is re-evaluating detente. Today we know better

than a few years ago that Soviet adherence to a policy of detente indicates a change in tactics rather than a change in strategy. In Soviet terminology, detente or "peaceful coexistence," does not mean "the cessation of the slogans about class warfare and about the 'ideological' conflict between the 'two systems' with the aim of replacing the capitalist (democratic) system by the communist system."[8]

This evaluation of the Soviet position is the heart of the present understanding of detente in the West. It stimulates demands that the West must also link its policy of detente to an offensive ideology. This can only be done if we succeed in combining three principles. I mean those principles which underlie the concepts of the "*demokratischer* Staat," the "*Rechts*staat" and the "*Sozial*staat."[9] Only in this way can the Western democracies be made attractive to the masses; only in this way will they win the ideological fight against communism and all non-democratic forms of socialism.

Although the ideological struggle between the East and the West is a special feature of the contemporary German scene, *Ostpolitik* in its present form is almost independent of this ideological perspective of detente.

## NOTES

1. Zbigniew Brzezinski, "The Deceptive Structure of Peace," *Foreign Policy*, No. 14, Spring, 1974, p. 40.

2. Hans Morgenthau, "Detente: Reality and Illusion," *The Wall Street Journal*, July 18, 1974.

3. Marshall D. Shulman, "Approaches to Detente," *Congress Bi-Weekly* (American Jewish Congress), March 29, 1974, p. 6.

4. Marshall D. Shulman, "Toward a Western Concept of Coexistence and Cooperation," *Foreign Affairs*, Vol. 52, No. 1, October, 1973, pp. 35-58.

5. Arthur J. Vidich, "Social Conflict in the Era of Detente: New Roles for Ideologues, Revolutionaries, and Youth," to be published in a special issue of *Social Research*, Spring, 1975.

6. Edward M. Kennedy, "Beyond Detente," *Foreign Policy*, No. 16, Fall, 1974, p. 21.

7. Pierre Hassner, "How Troubled a Partnership?," *International Journal* (Canadian Institute of International Affairs), Vol. 29, No. 2, Spring, 1974, p. 170.

8. "Detente: An Evaluation," *Survey*, Vol. 20, No. 5, 2/3, Spring-Summer, 1974, p. 1.

9. For an interpretation of the concepts of *demokratischer Staat*, *Rechtsstaat* and *Sozialstaat* (which are part of the FRG Constitution) cf. *Materialien zum Bericht zur Lage der Nation 1974* (Opladen: Westdeutscher Verlag, 1974), esp. Chapter II.

# DISCUSSION—Oct. 26 A.M.

**Q. MIROSLAV TODOROVICH,** *Bronx Community College*

At last night's session many points were made that the state of public opinion in the late 1930's was an important factor determining what the statesmen of the time could or could not do. Today you talked about detente and the realities in the Middle East. In your judgment, Professor Morgenthau, if and when another crunch occurs, and in view of the present state of our public opinion, will the United States be ready to discharge the proper role of a big power?

**A. HANS J. MORGENTHAU,** *Graduate Faculty, The New School for Social Research*

I share your concern, but I have no answer to your question. It may or may not. Who can tell what issues will arise which require a forceful reply from the United States, and to what extent the administration is willing to take forceful action and to what extent public opinion supports that action. What I am convinced of is that the Secretary of State is fully aware of the problem you are raising, and probably is as afraid as you are or as I am of the possibility.

**Q. RAËL ISAAC,** *Ph.D.*

Professor Morgenthau, you indicated that you felt that American policy in the Middle East was obscured by the use of the term "detente," and in fact this prevented America from actually following her interests there. Would you perhaps comment on what policy pursued by the United States in the Middle East might produce a genuine detente?

**A. HANS J. MORGENTHAU,** *Graduate Faculty, The New School for Social Research*

The point I was trying to make was that for a very short while, for a couple of days, our government thought that the Soviet Union would forsake its own interests in the

Middle East for the sake of detente, that it would act in the "spirit of detente." And our government was quickly disabused of that illusion. That is the only point I wanted to make. I did not intend to go into the substance of our Middle Eastern policy, except just to say that its main aim, its overriding aim, is the limitation, if not the expulsion, of Russian influence in the Middle East. Other moves are subordinate to that aim. I personally have great doubt that this policy will succeed. I am very much inclined to think that it will fail and the consequence will be another Middle Eastern war, again with the implications that such a war threatens a military confrontation between the United States and the Soviet Union. Of course, the point underlying all this is that detente, the whole topic of detente, is completely irrelevant to the actual issues which we are facing in the Middle East.

Q. SAMUEL HENDEL, *Trinity College, Conn.*

Professor Morgenthau, I am deeply concerned about the United States interests in the Middle East, particularly our concern to limit Soviet influence or possibly eliminate Soviet influence there. How do you deal with the argument that the best way to exclude Soviet influence in the Middle East would be for the United States to abandon Israel?

A. HANS J. MORGENTHAU, *Graduate Faculty, The New School for Social Research*

I am of course familiar with the argument, and the counterargument is that if the United States decided to do what this particular argument proposes to do, it would still be faced with the same kind of competition which exists today between itself and the Soviet Union. And the Soviet Union could still outbid the United States. So it would be a short-range advantage to the United States, but it would not change the overall competition because the assumption that the destruction of Israel would necessarily lead the Arab states to flock to the United States is simply wishful dreaming. On the other hand, you can say that in a confrontation not only between the United States and the Soviet Union in the Middle East, but between the Arab states and the United States, the latter would be considerably weakened if Israel were abandoned. In this respect the abandonment of Israel would serve the same function as the abandonment of Czechoslovakia by Great Britain and France in 1938. If you have a very optimistic outlook on the relations between the United States, on the one hand, the Arab nations and the Soviet Union, on the other, you can entertain at least the possibility of a policy of abandonment. If, on the other hand, you take a rather pessimistic view, it would be sheer folly from the point of view of the United States to pursue a policy of abandonment. But I would also say that our present policy aiming at competing successfully with the Soviet Union in the Arab world could never be successful if pursued at the expense of Israel. A year ago, I was pessimistic about the future of Israel. I am less pessimistic now. If I may prophesize in this respect: if Mr. Kissinger's policy fails, and I think it will, then another war is inevitable.

Q. SIMON HEAD, *The New Statesman*

Professor Morgenthau, would you care to extend your analysis of the policies to two areas you did not talk about. The first is the Soviet policy in South Asia. Do you see Soviet policy in that area propelled by the same political imperative as in the Middle East? Secondly, in the area of weapons, do you see Soviet leadership so highly influenced by the military to the point where they will strive for nuclear superiority?

A. HANS J. MORGENTHAU, *Graduate Faculty, The New School for Social Research*

The interest of the Soviet Union in South Asia meets two requirements of foreign policy. On the one hand, you may say it is the eastern extension of the traditional Russian Middle Eastern policy. On the other hand, it is the western extension of encirclement, the policy of encirclement of China. This is the main purpose of the Asian policy of the Soviet Union: to immobilize China so that she cannot expand and thereby threaten the whole Soviet Far East.

As far as nuclear problems are concerned, the Soviet Union is as aware of the absolute necessity, the literally vital necessity, of avoiding nuclear war. But in both the positions of the United States and the Soviet Union, there is an element of hope or at least of keeping alive the possibility that one or the other power might gain a first-strike capability which would mean the victory of one side over the other. I do not think this is articulated in the disarmament and arms control discussions of both nations, but I think it is implied in the whole competition itself. If you accept as axiomatic the absolute necessity of avoiding nuclear war, the fine points of superiority or inferiority in nuclear weapons are completely irrelevant—as long as both sides have the assured probability of destroying the other side which, of course, is assured on both sides many times over. So the competition, while it proceeds on a seemingly utterly irrational course, is justified by the expectation on both sides that there might be a way either to fight a civilized nuclear war out of which both sides might emerge alive, or to win a nuclear war by gaining such a superiority which, together with a surprise attack, might destroy the other side's capability of retaliating. There is ambivalence here on both sides which, I think, in good measure accounts so far for the failure of the nuclear disarmament negotiations.

Q. KLAUS PRINGSHEIM, *McMaster University, Canada*

Professor Morgenthau, one of the most widely discussed problems with regard to detente is the making of major concessions by the United States such as in the field of trade, the granting of most favored nation status, in the field of technology, the exporting of knowledge, or other similar concessions. Would you care to comment on whether the Soviet Union has made similarly valuable concessions to the United States?

A. HANS J. MORGENTHAU, *Graduate Faculty, The New School for Social Research*

In introducing my answer to your question, I want to say a word about why the Russians have launched upon detente. They have done so for three basic reasons. First, they are engaged in a struggle with China which both sides take with extreme seriousness. A Russian expert told me that a war with China is inevitable. This being the case, no country can afford a two-front confrontation, let alone a two-front war. In the measure that the relations between the Soviet Union and China become aggravated, the Soviet Union has a vital interest in mitigating the tensions with the West. Here is the first reason for detente. The second reason is that Russia has learned that a partially backward Russian economy cannot out of its own resources effectively compete with the highly developed Western industrial nations. Hence the need for the advancement of the quality of the industrial base of the Soviet Union. And the third reason for detente is to minimize if not to expel the influence of the United States from Western Europe—to emasculate NATO; to isolate West Germany and then to unify Germany under Russian auspices.

Because of the Soviet economic predicament, the United States is in a strong bargaining position, especially with regard to long-range credits and trade. The Soviet Union has recognized this and it appears to yield to American pressure on the question of immigration.

To answer specifically your question, namely, has the United States received anything to compare with its own concessions—is very difficult. The concessions on both sides are asymmetrical. The Russians, you may say, have made a concession by having allowed the United States to wage the last phases of its war in Indochina without interference, allowing it to disengage itself, allowing it to close the harbors and mine the larger rivers of North Vietnam. The Russians have also shown a certain restraint in the Middle East by not going as far as they could have gone. Here the fear of nuclear war is the overriding impediment. As you see, your question really cannot be answered exactly, because the relevant facts are not comparable.

Q. STEVEN WARNECKE, *The City University of New York*

Professor Morgenthau, you indicated that one of the Russian aims is to weaken the American position in Europe. The discussion so far has concentrated on the political and military aspects. I would like to address myself to the economic aspects, particularly the Trade Reform Bill of 1973. It seems that there is a destabilizing element as Europeans and Americans begin to compete for trade advantages with the Soviet Union and Eastern Europe. It is interesting to note that several articles in *The Wall Street Journal* described how this competition has developed in the machine and tool areas. It has also led to some tension within the European community because of the German advantage in this sector. I am wondering what your reaction is to this potentially destabilizing competition in the economic area?

A. HANS J. MORGENTHAU, *Graduate Faculty, The New School for Social Research*

There is no absolute unity in the Western camp. Since the end of World War II the Western camp has been united with regard to one issue only, namely, the containment of the Soviet Union. The different nations have followed their own policies in everything else. About fifteen years ago I made a survey to see on what issues all members of NATO would see eye to eye. I found only one issue. On every other issue at least one member pursued a different policy. So the idea of a united West has always been more of a dream than an actuality. It is natural that Western Europe compete with America for advantages in trade with the Soviet Union. The Soviet Union of course exploits that.

Q. PETER BAUER, *VWD German Economic News Service*

My question is addressed to Professors Morgenthau and Ludz. Is American detente policy endangering Western Europe? Three years ago there was a real hope in the Common Market countries for political unification. Professor Ludz, you indicated that any hope to achieve some sort of equality between the United States and Western Europe has been abandoned because of the energy crisis, American monetary policy, and Mr. Nixon's behavior at the energy conference in February when the French had the stamina to say no to any American energy sharing proposal. Has the policy of detente been arrived at over the heads of the Western Europeans, and at their expense?

A. HANS J. MORGENTHAU, *Graduate Faculty, The New School for Social Research*

Why was NATO created? In order to contain the expansion of the Soviet Union. If the leading statesmen of the United States and the Soviet Union attest each other their peaceful and noble intentions, obviously voices must be raised in Western Europe as to what the purpose of NATO is. If detente reigns supreme at the western frontier of the Soviet Union, what is NATO good for? If the relations between the United States and the Soviet Union are cordial, the reason for NATO's existence becomes dubious. This reminds me of Mr. Dulles' "agonizing reappraisal." We are not in Europe for sentimental reasons, but for reasons of national interest. And our troops in Europe are a political token of our determination to defend Western Europe. So in my view, and that of the present administration, any new withdrawal of troops would threaten to be a fatal blow to the political position of the United States in Western Europe.

A. PETER C. LUDZ, *The University of Munich; Graduate Faculty, The New School for Social Research*

I would like to add that any considerable withdrawal of American troops from West Germany will really threaten the whole detente business, and the whole of NATO. And there is a psychological factor. These West Germans are very very sensitive, and they are afraid that the Americans may withdraw even some of their troops. I think in this case it would be a kind of threat to NATO and to detente.

Q. ABRAHAM BARGMAN, *The City University of New York*

Professor Ludz, do you think the German leaders share Dr. Morgenthau's fears about the Middle East? To what extent is German policy limited to preserving that which has already been achieved through the European settlement and detente? Would their Europe centered policy interfere, for example, with the possibility of NATO reacting uniformly toward the Soviet Union's thrust in the Middle East?

A. PETER C. LUDZ, *The University of Munich; Graduate Faculty, The New School for Social Research*

I think the West-German government now has greater responsibilities, i.e., after the so-to-speak breakthrough on the international scene after the treaty with the Soviet Union. Our government is always saying that Bonn will not be involved in the Middle East because Germany, after all, is not a big power any more. It is a smaller state today with less political power, and Germany's attention is focused on the political unification of Europe and on preserving NATO in Europe. West Germany also has many difficult problems with the Arab countries. Hence it is better for West Germany to stay out of the Middle East. When Brandt and Schmidt talk about responsibility, they particularly mean responsibility in working toward the political unification of Europe.

Q. STEPHEN XYDIS, *The City University of New York*

Professor Ludz, would you care to comment on the reaction of the Chinese government to *Ostpolitik?*

A. PETER C. LUDZ, *The University of Munich; Graduate Faculty, The New School for Social Research*

I have no specific information besides what is being written in our papers. According to Mr. Kohl, the Chinese are very much in favor of the reunification of Germany. But what he tells us is not very important, because I think it was just in order to fight the Soviets so to speak. This has really nothing to do with the German question. The Chinese are interested in hitting the Russians wherever they can, and the reunification of Germany must be looked at from this perspective. I think there is no real political stand which the Chinese government has toward West Germany, or toward the German question.

STEPHEN XYDIS, *The City University of New York*

Thank you Professor Ludz. Your perception is interesting, but I do not think that it coincides with operational reality.


Q. ROSETTE LAMONT, *The City University of New York*

Professor Ludz, in Europe we heard people say this spring that the Soviet Union has betrayed Brandt. I would like to ask you whether people became fearful of a certain quality of politics, and whether the U.S.S.R. is unwilling to foster greater detente in fear of the possibility of a unified Germany?

A. PETER C. LUDZ, *The University of Munich; Graduate Faculty, The New School for Social Research*

The word "fearful" may be somewhat too strong. The Russians as well as the East Germans became somewhat afraid of the ambivalence of West German politics. On the other hand, I do not think that they are fearful that there will be a unified Germany. What they are afraid of is what they call "social democratism." This is what I have attempted to describe here when I spoke about the charisma of Willy Brandt, the Chairman of the Social Democratic party in the Federal Republic of Germany. The Russians are not fearful, but they are somewhat afraid of it, because the social democratic ideas have a very strong influence in East Germany. And, as you remember, perhaps, Chancellor Brandt was tumultuously greeted by the masses in East Germany and he became very popular there.

Q. WERNER CAHNMAN, *Rutgers University*

I know that ideological discussions are taking place in Germany. But I wonder, Professor Ludz, if you have not overemphasized this point?

A. PETER C. LUDZ, *The University of Munich; Graduate Faculty, The New School for Social Research*

I do not know if I have overstressed the ideological warfare in Germany. From watching the scene for many years there is, despite detente, going on a kind of ideological warfare emanating not so much from West Germany as from East Germany. One can say that this ideological warfare is very much linked to the present Soviet influence in Europe. Although there may be perhaps a relaxation of ideological tensions between the United States and the Soviet Union, there is no such relaxation between East Germany and West Germany. To fight effectively the East German political and ideological offensive, West Germany must counterattack by building a state based on three combined principles, namely, the *demokratischer Staat*, the *Rechtsstaat*, and the *Sozialstaat*.

Q. ABRAHAM MELEZIN, *The City College of New York*

Professor Ludz, did the German people make peace with the idea of the Neisse-Oder (Nyso-Odra) boundary line? I am interested in public opinion, and not the pronouncements of the government which may or may not reflect public opinion.

A. PETER C. LUDZ, *The University of Munich; Graduate Faculty, The New School for Social Research*

Independently of statements made by our government, I think it is quite clear that the West German public has made its peace with this fact of the post-war era. I do not believe that anybody in West Germany today expects a unification of West Germany with East Germany to take place, including all the former German territories now belonging to Poland.

Q. WERNER CAHNMAN, *Rutgers University*

What are the possibilities of East Germany taking over West Germany?

A. PETER C. LUDZ, *The University of Munich; Graduate Faculty, The New School for Social Research*

There is no danger that East Germany will occupy or take over West Germany because of the treaty and because of American influence in Europe. At the present time the Soviet Union is not interested in making the East Germans so strong that they can take over. Furthermore, East Germany is not so strong as it conveys to be, and hence there is no real danger taking over West Germany by East Germany.

Q. N. SETUNSKY, *Tass News Agency, Moscow*

My question is addressed to Professor Morgenthau. I wonder if the professor can give his opinion on how detente will continue to evolve under President Ford's administration.

A. HANS J. MORGENTHAU, *Graduate Faculty, The New School for Social Research*

This is a question for a prophet and not for a professor. I can tell you why what happened in the past was bound to happen. Some of my colleagues know exactly what is going to happen in the year 2000. I have my limitations.

# PART III
# DETENTE SINCE 1945,
# CONTINUED

# Imperialist Subsystems and Detente

## Erich Isaac

Detente in Europe has thus far been possible because acknowledged spheres of influence have been delimited. With the allied victory in 1945 the Soviet Union emerged as the most powerful state in Eufrasia, and the decades of the cold war, one can argue, were concerned with defining the limits of Soviet power. The Greek civil war and the various Berlin crises were, from a Western point of view, attempts to spread Soviet power beyond the spheres established at the end of World War II. This was described as a policy of containment by supporters of an active policy against communism or as brinkmanship by opponents, and in retrospect is taken by some revisionist historians as a manifestation of American imperialist intent. Nonetheless, the actual course of events could be described in terms that would have been familiar to the statesmen who settled Europe's fate at the beginning of the nineteenth century.

By 1960, at least in Europe, a certain stability was achieved, whether through action as in Greece, support as in Yugoslavia, inaction as in Hungary and later Czecho-slovakia, neutralization as in Austria, and so forth. The borders were not only defined but sometimes demarcated on the Soviet side by actual construction on the landscape, as for example the Berlin wall, minefields, dragon teeth and barbwire. But once demarcated a certain thaw became possible since not only the superpowers but the European states themselves accepted the legitimacy of the borders thus established. The importance of West Germany's *Ostpolitik* thus became that it bestowed legitimacy upon the last major border which had not been generally accepted by the West. In the resulting thaw the states of eastern Europe were able to achieve some measure of independence and freedom of development, and Western cohesion—both the cohesion between European powers and that between Europe and the United States—was conversely weakened. Strains in NATO were evidence of this and an actual, if thus far partial, breaking away in the case of France. You may therefore understand why I remain impressed by the judgment of the nineteenth century geographer Friedrich Ratzel who believed that geographically defined borders predetermine the possibility and the potential of political equilibrium.[1] This concern with concrete borders as with other aspects of political geography remains necessary to balance the more abstract analysis and systems of political science.

I concur with Professor Morgenthau that the relative abatement of American and Soviet confrontation was specific to Europe, allowing a policy now called "detente" to develop. In other parts of the world, notably Asia and Africa, the situation was far more complex. For here, even if great power willingness to honor an equilibrium had existed, borders lacked legitimacy from the perspective of the states themselves, most frontiers having been drawn by colonial powers with little attention to "national" or cultural realities. Rising state and national ambitions (not the same precisely because of the borders inherited from the colonial period) in the non-European countries meant that great power interests became inextricably involved with local power conflicts. This was all the more serious in view of the paradoxically greater power exerted by small non-European nations in an international climate that forbade direct intervention in their affairs. As Marshall Shulman has pointed out:

> . . .it is clear that the Soviet-American relationship is less the dominant axis of international politics than heretofore, and further, that the major transforming forces of the world are less subject to the control of the two superpowers than each had taken for granted in an earlier period.[2]

The Middle East is such a problem area because not merely is the location of boundary lines in dispute, but the very existence of one of its states is granted no legitimacy by those surrounding it. The situation is exacerbated because the withdrawal and decline of Western power in Asia has allowed imperialist ambitions, older and often much more explicit and conscious than the Western colonial drive of the nineteenth century, to rise anew and to press home their case through different levels of attack. Asian and African movements assert their spiritual superiority over an alleged Western materialism and desire for wealth and comfort. They are also nativist in the sense of declaring positive Western traits as original with them and denying outright past and present undesirable features of non-European cultures. All this, ironically, is presented in an amalgam of anti-imperialist terminology borrowed from our progressive or liberal intelligentsia or directly from Marxist-Leninism, which gives it great power in the West. Often the connection between Western intellectual sources and their Asian or African executors is, to be sure, purely verbal.

The justice of some of the accusations which are directed against Western colonialism may be conceded. This, however, must not blind us to the fact that imperialist traditions go far deeper in the ancient power centers of Asia than they go in the West and I would like to recall to you something so obvious that we no longer think about it, namely, that

Europe for the greater part of its historical existence was the target of invasions and recurring movements of colonization—the Turks reached Vienna in 1529—and not the originator of them. Although evidence for these imperialisms, the brunt of which are experienced at this time by other Asians and Africans, is manifest for all to see, the peculiar political and psychological vulnerability of Western intellectuals to the former colonials' charges has impaired their vision. In the words of the historian Henri Baudet: "the European" (I would say "the Western intellectual") "is shown to possess a psychological disposition out of touch with all political reality. It exists independently of objective facts, which seem to have become irrelevant."[3] The development of Western quasi-scholarly outlooks which elegantly equate aggression and defence, which evade unpleasant facts about Asian and African imperialisms, which have internalized the vast guilt literature beginning with Frantz Fanon and whose end is not in sight, have handed the architects of "third world" imperialism, to use a word from that vocabulary, a powerful weapon, for they can exploit the Western apologetic response to the accusations of Asians and Africans. This makes it difficult for the West to impose limits upon the aggressive policies of these "nationalisms" undermining the possibility of detente, which depends upon the recognition of limits to aspirations.

Non-European confrontations and conflicts will be resolved only when the realms of power are expressed geographically by demarcated borders whose inviolability is recognized. It is precisely because such demarcations have not occurred for superpowers and existing states outside of Europe that the subsystems, as some political scientists would call them, can exert independent force and even wind up as the tail wagging the dog. It is unfortunate that the study of frontiers has received so little attention and the subject dismissed with even better conscience today by those who argue, with utter folly, that modern weaponry has destroyed the importance of borders. It is well to re-

member the words of Lord Curzon, who was obsessed with
the need for establishing Asian frontiers, precisely because
of his desire for a "detente":

> Frontiers are the chief anxiety of nearly every Foreign Office
> in the civilized world, and are the subject of four out of every
> five political treaties or conventions that are concluded. . . .
> Frontier policy is of the first practical importance, and has a
> more profound effect upon the peace or warfare of nations than
> any other factor, political or economic.[4]

I do not wish to enlarge here on the recent oil crisis, but
only to point out that the Arab imperialist "subsystem" has
acquired a politically critical lever which will affect super-
power detente as well as the European state and alliance
system as it evolved after World War II. The intelligent
application of the oil weapon can bring about an effective
weakening of the social and economic fabric of the target
countries, which potentially include the United States. No
useful purpose is served by pointing to the relative weakness of the incipient Asian empires compared to the
super-powers. Nuclear capability has already been achieved
by China, nor is there any reason to believe that India,
after its recent nuclear advances, will refrain from nuclear
arms development. Similarly one cannot dismiss the grave
possibility that Arab states will acquire or develop or have
put at their disposal nuclear armaments and delivery systems. It is apparent that modern armaments of this kind
require a rethinking of our traditional approaches to the relative power of nations.

It is not simply a matter of detente being in danger. Detente produces dangers and we already see their effects. It
makes the conflicts of the subsystems invisible, except
perhaps to union leaders and journalists and some politicians, or, in so far as these conflicts are seen at all, they are
translated into anti-imperialist rhetoric such as "movements
of national liberation." Significantly, detente both blinds
and weakens those who might resist the resurgent im-

perialisms. Israel, for example, was caught so unprepared in 1973 in part because it relied upon detente to prevent a new onslaught. And now its intellectuals, who have internalized the reasoning of their Western reference groups, weaken its will to resist by adopting the same rhetoric toward the imperialisms that seek to destroy the state—the Palestinians are a "movement of national liberation" whose aspirations Israel must fulfill etc.

But the greatest threat of detente (not to detente), as Professor Eubank so well and lucidly pointed out, is that once this type of policy is embarked upon, so favored may it become in public opinion in democratic states, it seems unchangeable, undiscreditable, no matter what its dangers. The rest then follows, as Professor Herz described: appeasement, capitulation, surrender, finally war.

## NOTES

1. Friedrich Ratzel, *Politische Geographie* (München und Leipzig: R. Oldenbourg, 1897), pp. 447–470.
2. Marshall D. Shulman, "Toward a Western Philosophy of Coexistence," *Foreign Affairs*, Vol. 52, No. 1, October, 1973, p. 40.
3. Henri Baudet, *Paradise on Earth: Some Thoughts on European Images of Non-European Man*, trans. Elizabeth Wentholt (New Haven and London: Yale University Press, 1965), p. 8.
4. Lord Curzon of Kedleston, *Frontiers*, The Romanes Lecture 1907 (Oxford: The Clarendon Press, 1907), p. 4.

# Detente,
# the Middle East, and Oil

DANKWART A. RUSTOW

Since the title of the conference is "Detente in historical perspective," I should like to suggest three perspectives, drawn not from the history of Anglo-German diplomacy en route to Munich but from the histories of America and of Russia themselves, and of their mutual relations. Or rather, since my introductory perspectives must be brief, they will be mere glances at history.

First, I would invite you to take an overall glance at the history of the two countries that may or may not be currently in a process of detente. Both are continental countries that in several centuries expanded from the Atlantic, or some branch of it, to the Pacific—westward in one case and eastward in the other. Both attained their present boundaries late, the U.S. in the 1840's and Russia in the 1870's. Both are multinational nations, having displayed great powers of cultural assimilation—in Russia on the basis of a Great Russian patriotism tinged now with orthodox Christianity and now with heterodox Marxism; the U.S. on the basis of a very expressive version of the English tongue and some semblance of profession of the "American creed." This combination of continental expansion and cultural assimilation proved potent enough in each case to make America and Russia, in the wake of the two great European civil wars of 1914 and 1939, the undisputed global superpowers—undisputed, that is, except by each other. And considering the global scope of their interests it was no surprise that their contacts and conflicts ranged from strategic to diplomatic to economic to ideological; and the scenes of encounter from Berlin to Quemoy, Cuba, Vietnam, the Congo, and the Middle East.

The question before this conference, I take it, is whether and by what means these many tensions can be reduced or relaxed.

Thus far I have said little beyond what Tocqueville said better over a century ago; but for my second historical glimpse I can claim some originality. What is more, I have done the full documentary research myself, and the document concerning one of the most remarkable developments in Russo-American relations, not previously revealed by any historian, is page 68 of section I of *The New York Times* of Sunday, October 20, 1974. Two enterprising young coiffeurs on Madison Avenue—and I quote the document —"have come up with a series of Russian hairdos called 'detente.'"

What is to be admired is not just the up-to-date modishness of our beauty parlors in Manhattan, but also the sagacity of the young hairdressers in conceiving of detente not as a single phenomenon but as a theme with many variations.

One meaning of detente (as Professor Ludz rightly stresses elsewhere in this volume) is simply the acceptance of a quarter-century of the Pankow regime or Washington's belated acknowledgment of the existence of 800 million Chinese. Such simple acts of recognition can, of course, have complex implications such as the ability of the German governments under Brandt and Schmidt to play fully their European role, and in economic and financial matters even a role beyond Europe; or the greater flexibility that Kissinger's Chinese policy has given him in relations with Moscow—whether or not he always takes proper advantage of these possibilities.

Detente, secondly, may involve the creation of new facts—such as our withdrawal from Vietnam or the withdrawal of Soviet missiles from Cuba. Detente may mean the limitation of armaments or their partial reduction. And if such elements of detente are mutually negotiated, to echo Ludz once more, there is need of a shift of attitudes—of diplomatic flexibility, calm, and shrewdness until an agreement is concluded, and of vigilance and caution when it needs to be protected and preserved. The danger surely being, and here I agree with Morgenthau and other contributors to this volume, that public opinion in a democracy may be so elated over an agreement that it refuses to take note of its possible subsequent erosion.

Above all, there is need, as Hans Morgenthau has stressed in many of his recent writings and again in this volume, to examine the operation or non-operation of detente—its benefits and costs—issue by issue and region by region. Because of the wide range of American-Soviet interaction it is possible for the two countries to relax tensions in Europe while getting deeply embroiled in the Middle East —perhaps to the point of brinkmanship. It is possible for them to limit some arms while plunging into a headlong and perhaps uneven race in the development of others. Although in preparation for any top level diplomacy, such as Kissinger was off to in Moscow last October, it is essential to take these many facets of detente and non-detente together so as to explore any possibilities of improving the balance *quid pro quo*. But whatever the balance sheet, it always must consist of the separate and usually contradictory items on the ledger.

The debate as to whether detente as such is genuine or workable is usually so inconclusive because it really addresses itself not to one but to many questions.

And there is one other, more literal element of inconclusiveness: it often remains unclear for many years which side really got the better of a given bargain. And here I insert my third glance at the history of Russo-American relations. A century ago one of Mr. Kissinger's predecessors was widely denounced for having rashly purchased from the Czarist government a large tract of worthless tundra. But what in 1867 was known as "Seward's folly" in the last few years has turned out to be a wise investment toward partial energy independence.

Of all the separate current issues of relations between the

Soviet Union and the U.S., I should like to take up the effects of the Yom Kippur and oil wars; that is, I shall deal with the potential for detente in the Middle East.

Russian-American relations in the Middle East reached an extreme of tension in October 1973, but the situation has become extremely fluid, and it is by no means easy to register all the gains and losses.

The clearest gain (though no one knows exactly how solid or how durable it will prove to be) is the financial gain of Middle Eastern oil countries and of other OPEC nations as far away as Nigeria, Venezuela, and Indonesia. Canada, as a substantial oil exporter, has shared fully in the bonanza; and Russia might do so if it should give priority to oil export over domestic consumption, oil having long been a substantial source of foreign exchange for the Soviets. My own guess is that the OPEC cartel will not break at any early point and that prices will stay up into the early 1980's. The most solid gains, moreover, will be made by those countries that are populous enough and already developed enough effectively to absorb their oil earnings, such as Iran, Venezuela, Algeria, and Iraq, with less solid gains by the very poor and disorganized countries (Nigeria and Indonesia) and by the very rich countries (Saudi Arabia, Kuwait, Abu Dhabi and Libya).

The tab for this oil bonanza, of course, is paid by consumers in Europe, Japan, and the United States, and it is paid to the amount of $100 billion per year and going up. If there are any orthodox Marxists in Moscow they might well be forgiven for seeing in the resulting potential of financial and economic crises the approaching death rattle of capitalism. And if there are any social scientists here in America interested in precise definitions of fashionable jargon they may be forgiven for surmising that the phrase "post-industrial society" refers to America, Europe, and Japan after the Middle Easterners will have turned off the oil.

But a closer look at the realities makes me much more optimistic than such gloomy slogans would suggest. The U.S. has come out, or potentially can come out, of the oil and monetary crises far better than is usually assumed by the public—let alone by a government that wavers between Pollyannaish fantasies and "doomsday language," the latter being President Ford's own phrase.[1]

The U.S. remains the world's largest single oil producer, ahead of the Soviet Union and Saudi Arabia.[2] Moreover we possess such large amounts of coal and natural gas that petroleum only accounts for less than ½ (or 47.2%) of our energy balance, as against 59.5% for Western Europe and 76.4% for Japan. This implies tremendous possibilities of conservation of energy. Indeed, if we were willing to use only 1-½ times as much energy per capita as Europeans or Japanese, instead of 2-½ times as much, we would not need to import a single drop of oil.[3]

Three fourths of the petroleum sold in international trade, moreover, is paid in dollars (the remaining one fourth mainly in sterling), and this means that while Americans pay for imports in their own currency, Europeans and Japanese must work five times as hard to earn dollars if they are to keep importing the same amounts of oil as before. And since only one third of our oil is imported, as against virtually all of Europe's and Japan's, our competitors in world markets suffer a corresponding penalty. Finally, along with West Germany and Japan we remain the most attractive place for long-range investments once the Arabs will have fully mastered the arcane art of spending their surplus funds.

Several caveats must be added, however, to this generally optimistic account. First, the ability of American goods to compete favorably in the world market will mean nothing unless world trade continues to expand or at least does not drastically shrink. And since most world trade is among the industrial countries, this means that the troubles of coun-

tries such as Italy, Great Britain, France, and Japan will in-
directly affect other industrial nations, including the United
States.

Second, the American economy still is paying the deferred
cost of the Vietnam War and still suffering the consequences of Nixon's erratic stop-go economic policies so that
the impact of the petroleum revolution hit an American
economy already beset by inflation, unemployment, and
other troubles. The possibilities of energy conservation at
home and of financial leadership abroad will require reso-
lute and imaginative action. It remains doubtful, unfortunately, whether in the post-Watergate phase of American
politics either the President or Congress, or both in con-
cert, can rise to this twofold challenge.

Let me turn from this all-too-brief summary of the effects
of the recent petroleum situation to an examination of the
situation in the Middle East.

One of the chief consequences of the events of 1973/74
has been to loosen up, at least potentially, the tight and
rigid alignments of the previous two decades. Regional powers such as Saudi Arabia and especially Iran, through their
new oil wealth, have increased their stature on the international scene. Kissinger's tendency to formulate his Middle
East policies with a view to Saudi Arabian reactions, the
elaborate welcome accorded to the Shah in capitals such as
Canberra and New Delhi, and the election of an Algerian to
the Presidency of the United Nations General Assembly all
testify to this newly won stature.

The United States, in response to the brandishing of the
Arab "oil weapon," has switched from an extreme pro-
Israeli policy to a more "evenhanded" policy as between
Arabs and Israelis.[4]

Just how great American leverage on Israel will be in the
end remains to be seen. We can stop Israel from pursuing
her military advantage. ("I'm not sure the soldiers know it,"
Moshe Dayan explained to his countrymen in accepting the
cease fire at Suez in October 1973, "but the shells they are

firing were not in their possession a week ago."[5]) We can thereby bring her to the conference table. But it does not follow—and it is unlikely in view of Israeli and American electoral realities—that we can exercise any additional leverage so as to make her surrender interests she considers vital, such as a foothold on Golan, sovereignty in East Jerusalem, or rejection of a Palestinian state. Still, Israeli dependence on the United States, so vividly demonstrated last October, is today greater than at any time since 1947-48; and it would once again reach a maximum in any fifth round of full scale war in the Middle East.

Israel's dependence implied corresponding leverage for the United States in negotiating with the Arab countries—a constellation brilliantly exploited in Kissinger's airshuttle diplomacy—and a commensurate loss of Soviet power in the Middle East. Egypt, after nearly two decades of "occupation" by Russian technicians, seemed to relish its closer ties with the United States. With their newly found oil income, other Arab countries such as Algeria or Libya also were less susceptible to Soviet influence; even Iraq moved far out of the Soviet orbit. Russian influence, however, remained strong in Syria and even in Egypt, where new arsenals of Soviet weapons were building up, with implicit dangers of a new military outbreak; and further to the south in South Yemen and Somalia, with their strategic hold on the port of Aden and the strait of Bab el Mandeb.

The full story of the showdown of October 25, 1973, is not yet known. According to American sources, the nuclear alert of our NATO units stopped the Russians from dispatching a unilateral expeditionary force to Suez. If so, this amounts to a major U.S. gain in the balance between the superpowers; for power grows rusty unless it is applied from time to time in threats that are heeded. This may be the major explanation why the Soviets last summer were so circumspect in the Cyprus question, even though Greece and Turkey border directly on their sphere.

But the more fluid situation implies new opportunities

not only for Americans but for Russians as well. Greece and
Turkey, as members of NATO, have long been a potential
barrier between the Soviet bloc on one side and the Eastern Mediterranean on the other. But in the summer of
1974 Greece and Turkey were in a bitter dispute which did
not escalate into war mainly because the overall military
balance so clearly favored Turkey and because Greek forces
were too far from the scene in Cyprus. An immediate result
was Greek withdrawal from active participation in NATO,
with the future of American naval bases in Greece in
doubt. And even though the Cyprus question might
perhaps be settled on the basis of ethnic resettlement and
autonomy on the island, conflicting claims to offshore oil in
the Aegean provided continuing grounds for friction. The
major reason for Soviet reticence may thus have been a
cynical calculation that the continued conflict between Turkey and Greece can only benefit the Russians, whatever the
particular outcome.

As between Arabs and Israelis, too, the Soviets presum-
ably are interested in seeing the conflict continue. Israel's
presence has been the major single irritant in Arab relations
with the West, and the recurrence of war every decade or
so has made Israel's Arab neighbors heavily dependent on
Soviet arms shipments and military training missions. The
policy of letting the conflict smolder, moreover, is rather
easy to achieve. In the fall of 1974, for example, Arab
League recognition of the Palestine Liberation Organization
as spokesman for the Palestinians was quickly followed by a
statement by Foreign Minister Gromyko endorsing, for the
first time, separate statehood for the Palestinians. This public Soviet stand would make it difficult for any Arab government to accept any less. For Israel, Palestinian statehood constitutes a direct challenge to its existence so that
Arab intransigence on this point will virtually doom any
further efforts at overall settlement. With one stroke of the
pen Moscow thus was able to frustrate a year of Kissinger's
patient efforts, limiting him, at most, to negotiating further
partial withdrawals.

Russo-American relations in the Middle East thus have been very far from any actual detente. Rather, in a newly fluid situation there have been some gains, possibly only in the short range, for the United States and other gains, possibly for the longer range, for the Soviets. And, as the events of October 1973 indicate, the Middle East remains the one region where involvement by both superpowers can most easily lead to nuclear confrontation.

Both with regard to oil and to the Arab-Israeli conflict, the path of wisdom for United States policy is to accept the mixed effects of Yom Kippur and oil wars, and to use the room for maneuver that the present situation affords. We should keep trying to get the price of oil lowered; but failing that, we should be grateful if in the next five years it does not rise. We should curtail domestic energy consumption drastically, support the nascent International Energy Agency, and try to work out the recycling of oil dollars on a multilateral basis; but if no such multilateral solution emerges we should be prepared to attract a maximum of the oil funds so that we can undertake much of the recycling ourselves. We should keep trying to settle the Arab–Israeli dispute, piece by piece or as a whole; but failing that, we should be grateful if there is no fifth round of war in the next five years. In the Middle East as a whole we should accept what for two decades has been a fact: the coexistence of American and Soviet interests. Our maximum aim, therefore, should be a pattern of peaceful pluralism where there is room for both of these interests —but above all for independent local interests. But if it should prove impossible to achieve any genuine American-Soviet detente in the Middle East we should be grateful if in the next five years there will be no repetition of the heavy involvement and of the brinkmanship of October 1973.

## NOTES

1. Speech at World Energy Conference, Detroit, September, 1973.

2. In 1973 the United States produced an average of 9.2 million barrels of petroleum per day, as against 8.5 million in the Soviet Union and 7.3 million in Saudi Arabia. Since then production has declined slightly in the United States and increased in the Soviet Union. By the fall of 1974 there were reports that Russia had moved to first place.

3. For more detailed figures see my article "Who Won the Yom Kippur and Oil Wars?" *Foreign Policy*, No. 17, Winter 1974/75.

4. "Even-handedness" was the slogan proposed by William Scranton, former Governor of Pennsylvania, when he visited the Middle East on Mr. Nixon's behalf after the 1968 election. But the launching of this trial balloon was followed by larger arms deliveries and stronger diplomatic support for Israel than even under the preceding Johnson administration—until the reversal of course in October 1973.

5. Quoted, *The New York Times*, October 31, 1973, p. 16.

# Detente:
# An American Perspective

ARTHUR M. SCHLESINGER, JR.

There is a certain elusiveness evident in our discussion of detente. For detente is an amorphous, not to say cloudy, subject, and, like all clouds, susceptible to a variety of interpretations. Hearing experts argue about detente, one is reminded of the famous colloquy between Hamlet and Polonius. As you will remember, Hamlet, seizing Polonius by the arm, says, "Do you see yonder cloud that's almost in shape of a camel?" "By the mass, and 'tis like a camel indeed." "Me thinks," says Hamlet, "it is like a weasel." "It is backed like a weasel." "Or like a whale?" "Very like a whale."[1] But, whether camel, whale or weasel—and what three more appropriate images can define the cloud under discussion—this shapeless mood does retain some sort of reality. It marks, I think, a new phase in the evolution of the cold war, fully justifying both this conference and the debate about the meaning of detente that is taking place all over the world.

I suppose if one were to date the start of this mood, as far as the United States is concerned, it would really begin in the aftermath of the Cuban missile crisis. The forced withdrawal of Soviet nuclear missiles from Cuba meant the end of the forward policy identified with Khrushchev and made possible the movement away from tension expressed the next year in Kennedy's American University speech. This speech of 1963 formulated several major themes in the discussion of detente in the decade since:

—The recognition of a mutual responsibility in the cold war: Kennedy called on Americans to "re-examine our own attitude—as individuals and as a Nation—for our attitude is as essential as theirs."

—A belief that national interest, not ideology, is the fundamental determinant of policy: "However fixed our likes and dislikes may seem," Kennedy said, "the tide of time and events will often bring surprising changes in the relations between nations."

—A belief that the overriding national interest for both the Soviet Union and the United States in the avoidance of nuclear war, that in an era of nuclear plenty neither nation can destroy the other without exposing itself to destruction: As Kennedy said, "We are both caught up in a vicious and dangerous cycle in which suspicion on one side breeds suspicion on the other, and new weapons beget counter-weapons."

—There was the recognition too that detente would not by itself end the very grave differences between the United States and the Soviet Union. Detente does not require, as Kennedy said, "that each man love his neighbor—it requires only that they live together in mutual tolerance. . . . If we cannot end now all our differences, at least we can help make the world safe for diversity."[2]

This was the mood, first registered in the American University speech, that led Johnson, despite Vietnam, to attempt his bridge building exercises in Eastern Europe. Toward the end of the decade this mood became so powerful as to compel that most inveterate of cold warriors, Richard Nixon, to say that the era of confrontation had given way to a new era of negotiation.

That mood is powerful essentially because it is rooted in certain realities, because it does in fact respond to concrete national interests of the Soviet Union and the United States. The primary interest for both states remains the avoidance of nuclear war. Both governments had been compelled to stare down that particular abyss in October 1962, and I think both Khrushchev and Kennedy came away from that experience with a deepened sense of the horror for mankind should nuclear war ever break out.

In addition, there had developed in the Soviet Union in

the course of the fifties and more intensely in the sixties the obsession with China which led to an urgent need or an urgently felt need both to tranquilize the European front and to block any consolidation of a Chinese-American connection directed against the Soviet Union. The Russians doubtless anticipated that after the cultural revolution China for its part would be equally determined to block any Soviet-American relationship directed against itself, and that the Chinese would try to break out of diplomatic isolation. Indeed toward the end of 1968 signals began to come from Peking—signals which the Nixon Administration was soon in the happy position of being able to receive and return.

Beyond nuclear war and China, a third reason helps explain the Soviet desire for detente. That is, of course, the need to concentrate on national problems. Khrushchev's optimistic forecast at the beginning of a decade that the Soviet Union would catch up and surpass the West had failed. There consequently arose internal pressure to cut the arms budget and to attract Western capital, technology, and trade for purposes of internal development. I would not rate this motive as nearly so significant as nuclear war or China. I have no doubt that the Soviet Union could sustain its present level of defense spending without American capital and technology and trade. Still, other things being equal, external assistance would alleviate the domestic situation and give the regime a better chance to improve its appeal to the Soviet people.

Hans Morgenthau suggested that the Soviet Union wishes detente in addition in order to Finlandize Western Europe.[3] No doubt this is a favorite Kremlin pipe dream; but it seems to me more a speculative by-product of detente than a decisive cause for Soviet movement in that direction. It must be added that detente from the Soviet point of view has been sharply restricted to military and political matters. The Soviet resistance to what the Kremlin calls ideological co-existence has not relented. Any relaxation of ideological co-existence would obviously create a threat to the Soviet regime that is unacceptable to the Soviet leaders and incompatible with the present character of Soviet society.

As for the United States, there are strong reasons here too for the rise in the desire for detente. In addition to nuclear war, which, as noted before, is the supreme motive, there has been a recognition of a change in the nature of the threat that communism offers to the West—a change from the relatively coordinated international communist movement of Stalin's time to the disordered and fragmented communist world of today. In this polycentrist world, the extension of communism obviously no longer means, as it once meant, the automatic extension of Soviet power, or, for that matter, of Chinese power. For a time at least, the Soviet Union and China are more preoccupied with each other, more fearful of each other, than either is of the United States. The image of the Soviet Union in command of a world-wide movement orchestrating crises everywhere—guerrilla war in Vietnam, strikes in Venezuela, sabotage in Kenya and so on—which was the image in the high noon of John Foster Dulles no longer applies to the reality of the polycentric world.

Beyond that, the folly and shame of Vietnam finally brought home, I believe, to the American people, even perhaps to the American government, a sense of the limits of American wisdom and power in ordering the affairs of the world. In any case, it brought home the dangers of over-commitment; and it was accompanied by an exhaustion of the quasi-messianic impulse which had animated American foreign policy in the fifties.

All this is, of course, accompanied here, as in the Soviet Union, by an increasing sense of urgency about internal problems—problems which had been neglected as Presidents allowed themselves to be dazzled by the delights of higher diplomacy. I have in mind the question of racial justice in the early 60's, the question of disaffection and tur-

moil among the young in the late 60's, the question of inflation and depression today. All these have demanded a
much higher priority in executive attention and in resource
allocation than they had in the 1950's and 1960's. They argue
for greater presidential concern with the domestic community and a reduction in the amount of resources devoted to
the arms race.

I would say therefore that the detente mood has real
enough foundations for both nations. But the point is that
where detente has reality, it is because it is the expression
of a certain stability already achieved in the balance of
power; detente is the *recognition* of situations that have already come into existence. Detente, in short, is more a
consequence of power stabilization than the cause of it.
That is the reason, obviously, why detente prevails only
where the balance of power has reality, only where as in
Europe there are stable national units of power to be balanced, only where the force of circumstance has caused
both Moscow and Washington to agree on the balance for
other reasons. That is, of course, also why detente is much
less relevant, as Dr. Isaac pointed out,[4] to regions of the
world where power relations are, and are condemned to be
for an indefinite time in the future, in a condition of flux
and instability. In such parts of the world detente is at best
a wistful hope. Indeed the situation in these parts of the
world is in the main beyond Soviet and American control,
even if detente in Europe should result in wholehearted
Soviet-American collaboration elsewhere. The two superpowers together could not resolve, I believe, the problems
of the Middle East or the problems of East Asia. Such
problems have deep roots of their own and are far beyond
the joint capacity of the Soviet Union and the United States
to control.

The mood of detente thus arose in response to the power
reality of Europe. It has now established the framework for
a current national debate in the United States. The press
has reported the lineup in the executive branch as Secre-

tary Kissinger in one corner and Secretary Schlesinger in
the other; in the Congress Senator Fulbright in one corner,
Senator Jackson in the other. Now I do believe that, even
among these four opinionated figures, there is an important
measure of agreement as to the relation between the United States and the Soviet Union. They all agree, in principle at least, on the goal of bringing the nuclear arms race
under control; they all agree in principle on the advantages
of better commercial relationships; they all agree in principle on the importance of freer intellectual exchange; and
they all agree on the need for a continued vigilance with
regard to the Soviet Union. The argument is really over the
relative weight to be given to these various elements in the
actual scales of diplomacy and negotiations.

In the course of this debate, three broad positions have
emerged. The Kissinger-Fulbright position, I take it, is that
we should press forward as fast as practicable with the Salt
II talks and even take certain risks in the effort to bring the
arms race under control; that we should encourage trade,
bring the Soviet Union under the most favored nations
agreement and make it possible for American exporters to sell
goods in the Soviet Union; and that we should not press the
Soviet Union too hard over internal questions, such as the
treatment of intellectuals and dissenters or the denial of
Jewish migration.

The Jackson-James Schlesinger position, as I understand
it, is to move warily on Salt, to scrutinize every proposal in
order to see loopholes which might permit the insidious
Russians to take advantage of us, and in the meantime to
accelerate our own arms build-up even at the risk of pro-
voking a counter build-up on the part of the Russians. As
for the second and third questions—trade and human
rights—the Jackson position is to combine them and to require concessions on human rights in exchange for
economic assistance. Senator Jackson after his visit to China
seemed to lean toward a belief that we should support
China against the Soviet Union, but this is an individual ec-

centricity rather than an organic part of the Jackson-Schlesinger alternative.

The third position is roughly, for want of a better word, the liberal position, and would draw on elements of the other two. It is pro-arms control and pro-trade and in that regard sympathetic to the Kissinger-Fulbright position; but it is also pro-pressure on human rights and in that regard comes somewhat closer to the Jackson position.

Now the great difference between what I call the liberal position and the position of the administration is obviously on the question of human rights. This really goes to a deeper and more dramatic question; and that is what is the best way to liberalize Soviet society. (The administration view is that detente is more effective than pressure as a means of bringing about liberalization in the Soviet Union. The argument is familiar to us all—that continued tension can only prolong the siege mentality; but that reduction of tension, development of the economy, the improvement of living standards, in short, the spread of affluence would eventually strengthen the pressure toward democratization and in the long run alter Soviet society. Marshall Shulman has thus argued: "Over the long run, the cause of human rights in the Soviet Union will be most effectively advanced by a prolonged period of reduced tension, despite the immediate convulsive tightening of controls by the Soviet police apparatus."[5] It should indeed be noted that some Soviet dissenters, R. A. Medvedev among them, also make this argument.

Other dissenters take the opposite view, most notably Sakharov and Solzhenitsyn. They are skeptical about the "in-the-long-run" argument. They strongly doubt, as Sakharov has written, "that economic links will have inevitable consequences for the democratization of Soviet society."[6] They feel that, because the avoidance of nuclear war is in the Soviet interest too, the American government will not endanger political and military detente by speaking out against oppression. They do not think that, in asking the Soviet Union to behave like a civilized state, they are demanding (as Kissinger accuses them of demanding) "the transformation of the Soviet domestic structure."[7]

What is one to make of this debate? None of the questions involved is easily answered. Will detente and affluence produce a more liberal society in the Soviet Union? No one knows. Relatively high living standards did not save Germany from Nazism. On the other hand, the idea of the American government setting itself up as the moral judge of other nations suggests delusions of righteousness and crusades to reform mankind.

It is not to be supposed that concern about Soviet democratization is a sentimental question that hard-headed realists are right to ignore. Rather the contrary: the question of intellectual freedom seems to me at the heart of the stability of detente. As Sakharov has said, "Detente without democratization. . .would be very dangerous."[8] Detente without democratization would put the United States in the position of building Soviet economic and technological power and at the same time strengthening the Soviet regime's freedom to use that power without the constraints of internal criticism. The hard-headed fact is that it is difficult to trust a government that tries to forbid men like Sakharov and Solzhenitsyn, and Medvedev too, from speaking their minds. No doubt it is also difficult to trust the American government. But at least Americans are free to expose and condemn the lies of our own government. If freedom of speech offers no sure control of a government that wants to go to war, at least it lets the rest of the world overhear what the government's critics think its intentions are.

The liberalization of the Soviet Union would begin to move the world toward that common moral ground, that common framework of values and habits, which is ultimately the only way by which detente can deepen into genuine peace. Now, how is this to be done? The Jackson position favors intervention by the American Congress in the internal affairs of the Soviet Union through such means as the celebrated Jackson amendment. I find myself a little perplexed by this. As a traditionalist on foreign affairs, and as a student, in the broad sense, of Hans Morgenthau, I have always felt that reforming other countries is not the job of diplomacy. I still feel that the Jackson amendment is better as a threat than as a statute. On the other hand, the concessions the Soviet Union made for a time on the question of Jewish immigration persuaded the Jacksonians that our bargaining power in this regard was much greater than Kissinger appreciated. Yet how indignantly we would resent Soviet insistence that we reform our immigration laws or our racial practices in order to meet their standards! Plainly there were limits to the extent that the Soviet Union was prepared to swallow its pride in order to gratify Congress. In the end the Jacksonian insistence on public Soviet humiliation became too much for any great power to accept. The result was the Soviet cancellation of the trade accord of 1972.

This episode illustrates the dangers of growing dizzy with success. I am sure there are limits to the practicality of government intervention, whether by the executive or the legislative branches, in the internal affairs of another power. Because of this, I think it is all the more important that non-governmental voices be heard much more frequently and strongly than they have been on the question of human rights in the Soviet Union. I reflect with particular chagrin on the silence of the American Historical Association over the treatment of Soviet historians like Amalrik and Moroz. Richard Wade, our City University colleague, and I have been attempting for some years to persuade the AHA to pass resolutions condemning the treatment of Soviet historians. It's not that we anticipate that such a resolution would have tremendous consequence. But still, as the Soviet physicist Valery Chalidze said when Sakharov was under particular pressure, "I don't know how to defend Sakharov—I only know that you will never save anyone by silence."[9] No one can doubt that the spotlight of international attention on Soviet dissent does provide a restraint, and probably the most effective kind of restraint within our power, to save dissenters from what the regime would otherwise be tempted to do to them.

The early American Historical Association line, as set forth by the Executive Council at a meeting in September 1972, was that the Association should express concern about the fate of Soviet historians "only in cases where a general issue is at stake, namely the freedom of any historian to use responsibly gathered facts to arrive at a reasonable interpretation."[10] By this standard, as the then president of the AHA informed me, the organization would take no action about Amalrik, *et. al.*, on the ground that, as he wrote, they were "not being persecuted by the Soviet regime because of their historical activities but because they have been distributing clandestinely current information embarrassing to the regime."[11] It need hardly be pointed out that this is a shockingly restrictive standard and one, thank heaven, not employed by the National Academy of Sciences when it condemned the campaign against Sakharov, who was obviously not under persecution for his scientific activities.

Then came the case of Solzhenitsyn and *The Gulag Archipelago*. It is hard to deny that writing this book was an historical activity. The book has been highly praised by Medvedev, despite his differences with Solzhenitsyn on other matters, as well as by George Kennan and other Western scholars. It clearly falls within even the restrictive standard adopted by the American Historical Association in 1972. But the Association still remains mute. Instead of acting under the 1972 standard, the president of the Association inexplicably appointed a new committee to prepare a "position paper for early study by the Council."[12] One hopes that the American Historical Association is not waiting for historians to be drawn and quartered in Red Square before it decides to venture objections.

I am at a loss to explain this extraordinary behavior on the part of the historical establishment. It is doubtless related to what one member of the council described to me as the desire to preserve "collegial relations" with Soviet historians approved by the regime in a series of colloquia between American and Russian historians. As for the New Left historians, who for so long have paraded themselves as keepers of the professional conscience, they have invested so much of their historical judgment in the proposition that Stalinism was no worse than a bad cold that they may well fear that condemnation of Brezhnev's Russia would suggest that there were good reasons to oppose the Stalinization of Europe in the 1940's. This unaccustomed silence on the part of American radical historians compares most unfavorably with the forthrightness of the English radical historian, E. P. Thompson, who wrote recently, "We must make it clear again, without equivocation, that we uphold the right of Soviet citizens to think, communicate, and act as free, self-activating people; and that we utterly despise the clumsy police patrols of Soviet intellectual and social life. . . . Solzhenitsyn has asked us to shout once more. And we must, urgently, meet this request."[13] This is a request that the American Historical Association still declines to meet.

Still, cloudy and amorphous as the mood of detente is, it plainly marks a new stage in the cold war. So long as each side retains a nuclear retaliatory capacity the cold war has moved into a phase beyond military confrontation. I wholly agree with the pessimism expressed about the Middle East. But the Soviet Union has always been very careful—I wish we had been equally careful—about committing its own forces to combat beyond the direct defense of their own frontiers. I strongly doubt whether American and Russian forces are going to be meeting each other on the sands of the Lebanese desert. I think that the military considerations are now subordinate. I think it is foolish, for example, to suppose that the reduction of American NATO forces is going to tempt the Soviet Union, with unreliable satellites in front and China at the rear, into military adventures in Central Europe or the Middle East. Whether the Mansfield resolution or something like it is going to be passed this year or the next year or the year after, it is going to be passed; and Europe is going to survive. To say that the future of Western Europe hangs on the presence of two or three American battalions is to make that future much more precarious than I believe it is. The gravitational pull that Western Europe is going to exert on Eastern Europe is going to be rather more considerable in an open Europe than the gravitational pull of Eastern Europe on Western Europe.

But even though the military aspect of the cold war now seems to me at least decidedly subordinate, this does not mean that the cold war is over. That war in its most fundamental form is still with us today. Issues must continue between communism and democracy so long as the leaders of Russia and the leaders of China reject what is the essence of civilized society—the free discussion and exchange of ideas. Detente seems to me a valuable mood in which to have entered and an ideal well worth pursuing; but lasting detente requires a candid and open world. Otherwise, in the words of André Fontaine, detente is simply "the cold war pursued by other means—and sometimes by the same."[14]

## NOTES

1. *Hamlet*, Act III, Scene 2.

2. John F. Kennedy, *Public Papers. . .1963* (Washington: Gov't Printing Office, 1964), pp. 459–464.

3. In his remarks at this conference.

4. In his remarks at this conference.

5. Marshall D. Shulman, "Approaches to Detente," *Congress Bi-Weekly*, March 29, 1974.

6. Letter to Samuel Pisar, *The New York Times*, October 8, 1973.

7. Henry A. Kissinger, "U.S. Trade Policy and Detente," tes-

timony before the Senate Finance Committee, March 7, 1973, State Department release, 4.

8. *The New York Times,* September 5, 1973.

9. Valery Chalidze, "Two Men—One Exhausted, One Threatened," *The New York Times,* September 7, 1973.

10. Minutes of the American Historical Association Council meeting, September 29-30, 1972.

11. Lynn White, Jr., (president of the American Historical Association) to Arthur Schlesinger, Jr., October 24, 1973. Professor White was stating the views of the AHA Council.

12. Lewis Hanke (president of the American Historical Association) to Arthur Schlesinger, Jr., April 12, 1974.

13. Letters to *The Times* (London), September 13, 1973.

14. *Le Monde,* October 30, 1973; quoted by Theodore Draper, "Detente," *Commentary,* June 1974.

# Appeasement and Detente:
## Some Reflections

GEORGE SCHWAB

In the debate on appeasement and on detente a question has occupied my mind for some time, namely, why has so much attention been focused on the respective power political aspects involved and so little attention devoted to the ideological underpinnings of Nazi and Soviet politics. Surely, no one will deny the significance of power politics in either the Nazi quest for political hegemony in Europe or in the Soviet quest for hegemony there and elsewhere between 1939 (the Ribbentrop-Molotov pact) and the present. However, by stressing power and playing down or even ignoring the two ideologies, considered by the Nazi and Soviet leaders, respectively, to be true and absolute, a gap has opened up between the desires of liberal men and the political realities.

Despite the distinct political circumstances, a parallel may be drawn between the appeasers in London and the "detentists" in Washington. Both have approached politics as essentially void of ideological components, and have projected this conception of politics onto Berlin and Moscow respectively. But whereas the British appeasers had no knowledge of Germany and of German history and appeared not to have been inclined to broaden their horizon by becoming acquainted with Hitler's comprehension of politics,[1] the apparent chief detentist in Washington, Secretary of State Kissinger, as some of his writings show, understands politics as comprehended by the Kremlin.[2] But for reasons not entirely clear yet, in his political practice he shares a belief in vogue at this moment in the West, namely, that the politics of the Kremlin are mainly secular. In fact, the appeasers and the detentists have acted on the assumption that a basic consensus exists on the nature of politics between London and Berlin, and between Washington and Moscow. This is, perhaps, not an unnatural assumption if viewed in the context of the development of the modern European sovereign state.

As is well known, once the religious upheavals that had engulfed a part of Europe in the sixteenth and seventeenth century had been overcome, the modern European sovereign state began to assume definite shape. The decision on the part of European rulers to cleanse medieval public politics of ideological components was the most important factor in overcoming internal conflicts. This secularization of politics on the domestic scene had positive overtones in European interstate relations. That Catholic and Protestant rulers could finally accept the fact of belonging to the same family of Christians and thereby coexist enabled a public law of Europe to emerge.[3] Oppenheim was correct in observing that "by the end of the seventeenth century the civilised states considered themselves bound by a law of Nations, the rules of which were to a great extent the rules of Grotius."[4]

With only a brief interruption during the French revolution and the Napoleonic wars, the sovereign European state and the public law of Europe continued to unfold. As a result, wars waged during this period were a far cry from many of the public wars of the Middle Ages. No longer was the adversary, the enemy, conceived as a *foe,* i.e., as possessed by the devil to whom no quarter had to be given. The enemy was now considered to be a fellow Christian and, therefore, had to be treated accordingly.[5] Among other things, this entailed not abusing, and certainly not exterminating, prisoners of war, and even providing adequate medical attention to those in need. By also drawing distinctions between combatants and noncombatants, and between combat and noncombat areas, the public law further circumscribed the scope within which wars might be waged.

As long as sovereign states agreed on the prevailing notion of politics, they largely subscribed to the rules and regulations as contained in the public law. But once ideologies considered to be true and absolute were reinfused into politics, the public law received some mortal blows. For example, by utterly condemning the bourgeoisie and the entire bourgeois state structure, Marxist-Leninist ideology by definition also condemned the public law which had accompanied the development of the state. Although not basically anti-bourgeois, the hodge-podge of ideas underlying Nazi ideology, particularly the *Übermensch —Untermensch* distinction, was also hostile to the existing international legal system.

With the victory of one version of Marxism in Moscow, and with Hitler's accession to power in Germany, the politics of Moscow and Berlin, by virtue of their contamination with ideology, now possessed a sort of "surplus value" over secular politics to which the European states had gradually become accustomed.[6] To minimize or to dismiss for one reason or another the significance in international relations of politics fraught with ideology is simply to ignore stark reality which, in turn, may have most far reaching repercussions. This was certainly the case in the instance of the appeasers.

Moscow and Berlin, convinced that their respective ideologies embodied the truth, were certain that they were on the side of the future. Although the historical process would more or less automatically devour what they, particularly Moscow, considered to be anachronisms, it would not hurt to aid this process by pushing what was already falling. Translated into the conduct of foreign policy, this implied that the heretofore generally accepted public legal order was nothing more than a reflection of an overall rapidly declining era, namely, the epoch of the modern European sovereign state, and thus need not be preserved. Nevertheless, the very rules and regulations by which this legal order functioned could, in the name of a higher legitimacy, be exploited to undermine the hated system. Thus in contrast to those who have comprehended politics in a secular fashion, it is not surprising to what a considerable degree the Marxists-Leninists—and, in a somewhat lesser fashion also Hitler—have been preoccupied with the questions of strategy and tactics.[7]

As is well known, strategy is concerned with scoring the final victory in a grand design, whereas tactics deal with day to day questions on how to exploit particular situations.[8] Obviously, while strategy must never lose sight of the final goal, the tactics resorted to may, on the surface at least, sometimes even appear to contravene this goal. According to Lenin, it is absolutely essential for revolutionaries to analyze concrete circumstances and to act accordingly, and this, he insisted, precludes following "all abstract formulas and. . .all doctrinaire recipes."[9] For example, because of what he had learned during the abortive Beer Hall putsch, Hitler, in speaking of the tactic of legality as an instrument in his arsenal of weapons, put it as follows:

> When among our different weapons today we exploit parliament, this does not mean that parliamentary parties are there for parliamentary purposes only. Parliament for us is not an end, but only a means to an end. . . . We are. . .a parliamentary party. . .only out of necessity. . . . We do not battle for parliamentary seats for the sake of such seats, but in order to liberate one day the German people. . . . The constitution prescribes only the ground on which the battle has to be fought, not its aim. We enter into the legally constituted bodies and we shall thus make our party the decisive factor. Once in possession of constitutional rights, we shall then forge the state into the form of which we approve.[10]

Leaders of totalitarian one-party states have kept strategy and tactics distinct in international politics as well. The effect is often to confuse, dumbfound, neutralize, and hood-wink a wide spectrum of opponents. Thus, Hitler, while making aggressive moves in Europe, confused his oppo-nents by, among other things, speaking the language of the League of Nations,[11] and signing all sorts of treaties (and then breaking these when they no longer served his purpose).[12] According to Rauschning, Hitler observed in this context that his party comrades "'will understand pre-cisely what I mean when I speak of world peace, of disar-mament, and of security pacts.'"[13] In the words of Bullock, "these were the tactics of legality applied to international relations. . . ."[14] Hitler's success in forging a *Grossraum* was due in part to his ability to hoodwink his opponents and, in particular, because the appeasers in London chose not to comprehend Berlin's political signals.

In reflecting on the history of the period, one cannot help but be reminded of Hegel's observation that at times it is difficult to distinguish where tragedy ends and comedy begins. Had it not been for the tragedy which embraced the world, one could easily imagine oneself sitting back at a version of Berlin's *Kabarett der Komiker* and roaring with laughter at Chamberlain's reactions to Hitler. In discussing the trustworthiness of Hitler just two days before signing the Munich agreement, Chamberlain noted that "I believe he [Hitler] means what he says when he states that."[15] It is also said that Chamberlain remarked on his death bed that things would have turned out differently if only Hitler had not lied to him.

By the end of 1938, Germany, in relation to the other European sovereign states, was probably the strongest polit-ical and most modernized military state in Europe. Based on his strength, Hitler felt prepared to start acquiring what he had considered to be the much needed *Lebensraum* for Germany. Hence, early in 1939 he made his first territorial move outside the periphery of German-speaking peoples.

The public outcry following the dismemberment of Czechoslovakia in March 1939 was largely responsible for the appeasers taking another look at Hitler. Appeasement, which had really begun with the Anglo-German naval a- greement of June 1935, had in fact, if not yet in theory, run its course by April 1939.[16] By then it was clear that the only way to stop Hitler's aggression would be to engage Germany in a war, whereas at the time of Hitler's re- militarization of the Rhineland, a police action would have sufficed. By having failed to comprehend the ideological com- ponents Hitler had injected into politics, the appeasers were unable to grasp his strategy, and they were usually also puzzled by his tactics. For their political naiveté the world was forced to pay a heavy penalty.

Detentists, and even decided critics of Washington's pol- icy, as, for example, our distinguished colleague and friend, Hans Morgenthau,[17] now project onto the Kremlin a secu- lar notion of politics. Has Moscow abandoned the Marxist- Leninist components of its politics? To what extent is Mos- cow paying lip service to Marxist-Leninist doctrines?

Unfortunately, I belong to a small minority who are not yet prepared to share the belief that Moscow has discarded the general principles of its political theology, and that Marxist-Leninist doctrines are little more than cosmetic facades. A careful examination of the question of peaceful coexistence in communist literature reveals a consistency of view from Marx to Brezhnev on the ultimate impossibility of the various systems coexisting.[18] The only thing that changes from time to time are the tactics resorted to in helping the historical process push what is already falling.[19] By assuming that Moscow is sincerely interested in follow- ing a genuine course of detente, our detentists are misread- ing Moscow's political signals, and have, thereby, seen only what Moscow at this moment wishes to convey to the West.

If detente means the easing of political tensions, which also implies military ones, one often wonders if the word is at all applicable to what is emanating from Moscow.[20] If we look at detente from Moscow's perspective, rather than from preconceived and locked-in positions now fashionable in the West, it can be understood as a necessary tactic emanating from Moscow's rivalry with Peking. (Were this rivalry resolved tomorrow, the West would then be faced by other tactics.)

Ever since China emerged as a troublesome neighbor and one whose nuclear arsenals and delivery systems are growing and improving, Moscow has been forced for tactical reasons to open more channels of communication with the West. Soviet military strategists cannot discount the possibility of a military invasion of the Warsaw pact countries, including perhaps the European part of Russia, at a moment when Moscow may find itself in a military confrontation with Peking. To foreclose such a possibility, the Kremlin has followed in this so-called period of detente two tactical courses which on the surface may appear contradictory, but in fact form two sides of a coin. Whereas the Kremlin's military aim is to weaken the western part of Europe and the United States, Moscow is simultaneously enticing the West to extend credits, export western technology, and expand trade with Russia.

Bearing in mind that Western Europe could serve the United States as a launching platform to stab the Soviet Union in the back while its hands are tied by a military confrontation with China, Moscow has continuously and diligently expanded its military posture in Europe.[21] This is in contrast to the continual weakening of NATO. One may thus begin to wonder—however far fetched this may seem—whether the position Washington appears to have locked itself into, namely, that the Soviet Union has no military designs on Western Europe, reflects political reality as viewed from Moscow, which is more conscious of the historical process than we are. Could it be that Moscow is preparing for the eventuality of a rapprochement with Peking?

Let us return to one of Moscow's immediate tactics, namely, to minimize the threat of Western Europe's serving as a launching platform for a military invasion of the Warsaw pact countries. It is essential for Moscow to be able, at the critical moment, to cut Western Europe off from the United States. Because the United States Air Force simply lacks the planes to ferry hundreds of thousands of soldiers across the ocean in a short span of time, not to speak of supplying them in addition, the only option open to the United States is the sea route. It is in this context that one may explain the expansion and modernization of the Soviet submarine fleet in particular.[22] To encircle Europe the Soviet Union is putting much emphasis on its naval contingents in the Mediterranean and the Baltic. Originating at almost opposite ends of the world, both contingents at the critical moment would converge somewhere in the vicinity of Gibraltar, and thus blockade Western Europe.[23]

Even if we disregard the Soviet Union's encouragement of Egypt and Syria to attack Israel in 1973, and Moscow's support of the Arab oil blockade,[24] the expansion of Soviet military might in Europe is sufficient evidence that in so far as the Kremlin is concerned, detente for Moscow has an entirely different meaning than it does for us.[25] In the light of the evidence introduced, it is hard to share Professor Morgenthau's statement in *The Wall Street Journal* that *Ostpolitik* "has created *genuine* detente at the very focus of the Cold War,"[26] or Professor John Herz' assertion that *Ostpolitik* has created "a new basis for peace and stability in Europe."[27] Even if we were to grant that a consensus exists on the nature of politics between the West and the U.S.S.R., in view of the Soviet Union's military posture in Europe and in the Eastern Mediterranean, can a genuine detente in today's world really be divisible, i.e., can it exist in Europe and not in the Middle East? At least the military alert of 1973 certainly militates against such an interpretation.

Expansion of trade, credits, and the exportation of western technology is as a rule a healthy economic sign in itself, and something which could lead to an interlocking dependence of the technologically advanced societies. Reiterating the notion that the "business of America is business," corporation executives in their eagerness for profits do not appear to be concerned with the political implications of their transactions. This attitude is, as a rule, highly welcome, particularly in instances where business transactions occur among politically rather homogeneous societies. It is even welcome in the instance of heterogeneous societies which are neither actual threats nor, for obvious reasons, potential threats to the world.

But the matter is entirely different with the Soviet Union. From Moscow's perspective, trade, credits, and technology are not viewed as they are in the West, primarily in economic terms, but rather in political terms. Yet by viewing Moscow's eagerness for economic, industrial, and technological cooperation as ends, rather than as means, detentists and the business establishment are misreading Moscow.

For detente to succeed, in the words of Keith Eubank, it requires "reciprocity, sincerity, and agreement on the basic issues."[28] This, unfortunately, is not the case now. Hence, in conclusion, let me simply state that we are confronted by a dilemma. What alternatives do we have? Total appeasement, which could conceivably lead to the Finlandization of the United States;[29] partial appeasement, which could lead to grave miscalculations on the part of Moscow as was the case in 1939, or a return to the relatively drawn lines of the immediate post-war period.

The course least likely to be pursued by Washington is also the course least likely to provoke a nuclear confrontation, namely, outright appeasement. The course we follow now can best be summarized as partial appeasement because, in our reactions to the challenges emanating from Moscow, we are permitting the Soviet Union to gain ground at the expense of our political posture. (Letting dissidents leave can in the long run only help the Soviet Union in resynchronizing its society, but in the meantime Russia can score vital economic, industrial, and technological gains.) Unless this course is permitted to culminate in total appeasement, the current largely one-way relationship cannot go on for too long without some sort of major confrontation. Hence, gradually and sternly, we have no choice but to draw specific lines, with the clear understanding that any attempts to breach these will be met by a determined stand.

## NOTES

1. See A. L. Rowse, *Appeasement: A Study in Political Decline, 1933-1939* (New York: W. W. Norton & Co., 1963), pp. 19-20; Martin Gilbert and Richard Gott, *The Appeasers* (Boston: Houghton Mifflin Co., 1963), p. 26.

2. Henry A. Kissinger, *American Foreign Policy: Three Essays* (Expanded ed.; New York: W. W. Norton & Co., 1974), pp. 34-39; *The Necessity for Choice: Prospects of American Foreign Policy* (New York: Harper & Brothers, 1961), pp. 172-173; *Nuclear Weapons and Foreign Policy* (New York: Harper & Brothers, 1957), pp. 321-326.

3. A most perceptive discussion of the emergence of the public law of Europe which accompanied the rise of the sovereign state is Carl Schmitt's *Der Nomos der Erde im Völkerrecht des Jus Publicum Europaeum* (2nd ed.; Berlin: Duncker & Humblot, 1974), pp. 112-185.

4. L. Oppenheim, *International Law: A Treatise* (Edited by H. Lauterpacht; 8th ed.; London: Longmans, Green, & Co., 1955), Vol. I, *(Peace)*, p. 85.

5. For a discussion of the conceptual distinction inherent in the words "enemy" and "foe," and for some of the political implications of the terms in antiquity, in medieval and modern Europe, see George Schwab, "Enemy oder Foe: Der Konflikt der modernen Politik," (Translated by Jutta Zeumer), *Epirrhosis: Festgabe für Carl Schmitt* (Berlin: Duncker & Humblot, 1968), Vol. II, pp. 665-682; see also Ion X. Contiades, " 'ΕΧΘΡΟΣ' und

'ΠΟΜΕΥΙΟΣ' in der modernen politischen Theorie und der griechischen Antike," *Griechische Humanistische Gesellschaft*, Athens 1969, pp. 5-28.

6. Although the ideological components which until recently were embodied in American politics cannot be dismissed as having helped to undermine international law, it must also be remembered that American foreign policy did not play a major role in Europe between 1933 and 1939.

7. Originally the theorizing on both occurred while the respective totalitarian movements were struggling to capture power. Once in possession of power the lessons learned, with variations on a theme of course, were transferred to the domain of international politics.

8. The distinction drawn by von Clausewitz in his *On War* (Vol. I, 2,1 and 3,1) serves as a crucial point of departure for totalitarian movements in their quest for power and also for totalitarian one-party states in their conduct of foreign policy.

9. V.I. Lenin, "Guerrilla Warfare" (1906), *Collected Works* (Moscow: Foreign Languages Publishing House, 1962), Vol. 11, pp. 213, 214. See also Lenin's " 'Left-Wing' Communism, An Infantile Disorder" (1920), *ibid* (1966), Vol. 31, pp. 96-97.

10. As quoted by the *Frankfurter Zeitung*, September 26, 1930.

11. See Hermann Rauschning, *Gespräche mit Hitler* (France: Europa Verlag New York, 1940), p. 108. See also Hitler's famous Peace Speech of May 17, 1933. Reprinted in *The Speeches of Adolf Hitler, April 1922—August 1939* (Edited by Norman H. Baynes; New York: Howard Fertig, 1969), Vol. II, esp. pp. 1046-1047; also Hitler's interview of October 18, 1933, with a British correspondent. *Ibid.*, pp. 1105-1108.

12. Rauschning, *Gespräche. . .*, pp. 106-107.

13. *Ibid.*, p. 108.

14. Alan Bullock, *Hitler, A Study in Tyranny* (Rev. ed.; New York: Harper Torchbooks, 1964), p. 324.

15. Neville Chamberlain, *In Search of Peace* [New York: Reprinted by Books for Libraries Press, 1971 (Essay Index Reprint Series)], p. 197.

16. Many appeasers were convinced of the necessity of continuing to cooperate with Hitler and to facilitate this they were prepared to accommodate him on the question of Poland. See

Gilbert and Gott, *The Appeasers*, pp. 248-260. See also above, Keith Eubank's "Detente 1919-1939: A Study in Failure," p. 21.

17. See his "Detente: Reality and Illusion," *The Wall Street Journal*, July 18, 1974.

18. See "Detente: An Evaluation," *Survey*, Vol. 20, nos. 2/3, Spring-Summer 1974, pp. 1-3; Josef Korbel, *Detente in Europe: Real or Imaginary* (Princeton: Princeton University Press, 1972), p. 17.

19. See N.S. Khrushchev, "Report of the Central Committee of the Communist Party of the Soviet Union to the Twentieth Party Congress" (February 14, 1956), *On Peaceful Coexistence: A Collection* (Moscow: Foreign Languages Publishing House, 1961), pp. 7-14. See also Robert C. Tucker, *The Marxian Revolutionary Idea* (New York: W.W. Norton & Co., 1970), pp. 140-160.

20. Korbel puts his finger on this when he speaks of "detente: a problem of perception." *Detente. . .*, pp. 31-39.

21. See Drew Middleton, "Amid Detente, Soviet Military Expansion," *The New York Times*, July 1, 1974; also, the studies pouring forth from the Institute for Strategic Studies at London, in particular, *The Military Balance, 1972-1973* (1972), pp. 86-91.

22. It is interesting to compare the 1973/74 edition of *Jane's Fighting Ships* (pp. 529-530) with previous editions; see also, *The Military Balance*, pp. 91-92.

23. According to Eugene V. Rostow, "The Middle Eastern war of October, 1973, was a fundamental Soviet thrust at the North Atlantic Treaty Organization, designed to outflank allied forces in Central Europe; separate Europe from America, and bring Europe's resources under Soviet control; and drive the United States out of the Mediterranean and Europe itself." "Western Non-policy on Oil and the Middle East," *The New York Times*, October 21, 1974.

24. The grave impact oil prices have on western economies is surpassed only by the political complexities of the world situation. It is not at all inconceivable that, in return for some sort of behind the scenes promise from Washington as regards Peking, the Soviet Union may look aside at an American military landing in one or more of the Arab oil producing countries. In the absence of some behind the scene signal I doubt whether Kissinger would have thought it wise suddenly to threaten the Arabs on the question of oil.

25. On the evolution of the meaning of this term see "Word 'Detente' Has Intricate History," *The New York Times*, June 28, 1974.

26. *Op. cit.* Italics added.

27. See above, pp. 35-36.

28. See above, p. 23.

29. It is not inconceivable that, as a result of another confrontation in the Middle East, in which the Arabs may again resort to their oil weapon, some of our allies in Europe may feel so squeezed between the Soviet posture and Arab oil power that they may drastically curtail their ties with the United States. What the Soviet Union has so far failed to achieve, namely, an all around Finlandization of Western Europe, the Arab oil producing states are now capable of doing. In short, without firing a shot they have the capacity of closing the casket and hammering the nails into the coffin.

# DISCUSSION—OCT. 26 P.M.

Q. PETER BAUER, *VWD German Economic News Service*

Professor Rustow, why do you consider the oil-sharing agreement positive? I don't look at it in positive terms at all. If you bear in mind that the Europeans have a sixty-day supply, that they have no oil resources, that North Sea oil will be available in quantities only in the 1980's, and that another oil embargo may be directed at both Europe and the United States, then you come up with a positive approach. We would be using your oil. Would the United States be willing to give it to us with a long supply line? Is there enough oil? Basically the answer is no. What the energy crisis has done is to split Europe. Incidentally, American policy had tried to accomplish this in the last three or four years—splitting up Europe, making us small again, after you experienced in '70 and '71 how powerful an economic entity like the Common Market could be. With the energy crisis we are reduced to little puppets again, and I think that Kissinger seems to enjoy now the state of affairs we are in.

A. DANKWART A. RUSTOW, *The City University of New York*

There are a few factual errors on the oil storage question in Europe. The aim announced by the Common Market long before the crisis was ninety days. This was not attained in all cases before the crisis, but now it has been attained and surpassed. The Germans are developing an oil storage program in their salt mines, and that will add to their capacity—I think up to one hundred and five days. Secondly, if the Middle Eastern countries were to cut off oil both to Europe and to the United States, in that situation the sharing will be automatic. Plans for sharing are necessary once people are singled out, not when they are all in the same boat anyhow. The third thing, and this I found very surprising and would have thought impossible beforehand. The agreement does provide for the United States not precisely to export oil to Europe in any situation, but if a European country should be singled out, the pool on which calculations are based includes the total United States oil supply, domestic and imported rather than just the imports. This is a major American concession. Let me conclude by observing that this is the first major positive step in a new area. The Common Market started out with an attempt at unifying coal and steel just when coal was getting off the market and becoming seemingly obsolete in favor of oil. So there was an attempted energy policy that died while it was being born because coal died out. Then there was a unification of agricultural subsidies. These —other than customs union—are the two concrete things the Common Market has achieved in the way of commonness. There is I think now the possibility of achieving some common policy on energy, but it will take just as long as any of the others did before. It is a five to ten year process, and it may also lead to a unified monetary policy as a result of the new pressures on the financial system.

Q.  HERBERT STRAUSS, *The City College of New York*

Professor Rustow, your presentation seems to contain a contradiction in conceptualization or analysis. On the one hand, you discuss the interdependence of global issues. On the other hand, you separate the issues piece by piece. The difference between members of the panel is that one of you sees possibilities of detente in one area, while the other sees the basic principle of Soviet policy at work which affects detente everywhere.

A.  DANKWART A. RUSTOW, *The City University of New York*

One has to separate the issues and take them one by one and then in conclusion stress the interdependence of issues. I do not believe that there is a contradiction in my position. It seems to me that economic issues interrelate themselves through the normal working of the world-wide economy to the extent that the countries are in international trade —which of course excludes most of the communist countries. Specifically on oil, an oil shortage directed at any country gets distributed world wide through the kind of interconnecting activities of the oil companies. Political issues are less interdependent. It is quite possible to have disarmament at the nuclear level and rearmament at the conventional level, or war in the Middle East and peace in Europe. What Kissinger ought to be doing ahead of time when he goes to Moscow is to draw up a balance sheet and see where some issues might be connected that it is to our advantage to connect in the negotiations, even if they could theoretically go on separately.

Q. PETER BAUER, *VWD German Economic News Service*

Professor Schlesinger, you made a remark that the state of affairs in Europe is very precarious. If I look at Professor Schwab's documentation of the Soviet military presence in Eastern Europe, and in view of the non-proliferation treaty, the lack of an effective French delivery system and also of a British one, and the possibility of an American troop withdrawal—confronted with this situation, how do you believe the Europeans will react toward the Soviet Union? If they cannot trust the one power that has weapons to protect them, which is not willing to share them (you know that you have 7000 nuclear warheads on European soil but they are all under American control), I would like to find out how you view the overall situation.

A. ARTHUR M. SCHLESINGER, JR., *The City University of New York*

I may of course be wrong but I would imagine that a Soviet military invasion of Western Europe would rate about 946 on the Presidium's list of current priorities. If the Soviet Union were seriously bent on such invasion, I doubt whether it could be deterred by the presence of some American troops. The basic question is whether the United States feels it has an interest in Western Europe worth defending. If it does feel that, it will react whether or not it has any troops there. If it does not feel that, it will not react whether or not it has any troops in Europe. The controlling question is whether we have such an interest. Historically we have always regarded what Jefferson called in 1814 the gathering of the force of Europe in a single hand as a threat to the United States. I imagine this would continue to be the American view. Of course, nuclear weapons complicate matters. It is a difficult question to answer whether the preservation of a non-communist Western Europe is going to be worth the destruction of New York. Again, this will not be affected by the level of current military deployments. If it is decided that the exposure of the United States to nuclear destruction is not worth it, that will be a decision made quite independently of American force levels in Europe. The question of the current force level in Europe is of relevance only in relationship to the morale of the Western Europeans. They are perfectly capable of increasing their own military contributions. I do not consider the decision about force levels of American troops an important decision. Should a grave threat develop in Europe, American troops could return in force.

Q. RENÉ ALBRECHT-CARRIÉ, *Columbia University*

In his careful analysis Professor Schwab raised an interesting question about ideology. Nobody really knows what goes on in the Kremlin. I would just like to mention one thing. Some time ago there was a great revolution in France and for a while during the nineteenth century that ideology was absolutistic, universalistic, etc. It had some of the same qualities as the Marxist ideology, but in time this ideology became diluted. We hear the same kind of argument now about communist parties in Italy or France or some other places. I think there is a very good chance that the process is repeating itself.

A. GEORGE SCHWAB, *The City University of New York*

Unfortunately we do not have time to go into a discussion

of the implications which the ideological components of French politics had toward the end of the eighteenth century and in part of the nineteenth century. What strikes me in the instance of the Soviet Union is the extent to which Soviet leaders more than fifty years after the Revolution continue to pay attention to ideology, strategy, and tactics. What concrete evidence do we possess that the Kremlin has embarked on a revisionist course? The fact that the Soviet Union is at this moment conveying a specific image of itself is not necessarily an indication that it has compromised on the fundamentals of its ideology.

Time and again Lenin stressed that good revolutionaries must be cognizant of reality and hence avoid operating in a vacuum. Thus, in so far as tactics are concerned, revolutionaries must be prepared to play the bourgeois game—not as an end, but as a means. A lesson can be learned from the diatribes between Moscow and Peking of some fifteen years ago. Counterattacking the charge of revisionism, the Kremlin accused Peking of orthodoxy, of suffering from left-wing infantilism. But given the world situation, particularly Moscow's realization of the consequences a nuclear confrontation may have on the Communist world, I think that Khrushchev was a better tactician in the Leninist sense of the word than his counterpart in Peking.

As regards Western Europe, the Soviet Union has scored impressively. No matter what arguments are presented to the contrary, the West European sovereign states, or whatever is left of their respective sovereignties, are vis-à-vis the Soviet Union Finlandized. Because a criterion of politics is the ability on the part of the sovereign to decide who the enemy or the foe is and to act accordingly, neither Bonn, Paris, or London is capable, without the United States, of deciding today that Moscow is either the enemy or the foe and to act in accordance with that decision.

In so far as Communist parties in France and Italy are concerned: are they or are they not reformist? The evidence indicates that they are more reformist than the other way around. However, their reformism may turn out to be tactical maneuvers. Only time will tell.

ARTHUR M. SCHLESINGER, JR., *The City University of New York*

Incidentally, whether France or Italy go Communist is a question that is really beyond the solution of the United States. If that is really the way Europe wants to go, that is the way Europe wants to go and we cannot stop it. I do not believe Europe will go in that direction. Judging at least by some of the reactions not so much in the French Communist party as in the Italian Communist party, it may be that the Italian party does not want to become a satellite party. The power of nationalism to mould communism to its own purpose as seen in other parts of the world is not perhaps to be excluded from the European consideration. I think one thing we have learned is the limits of our powers to decide the destiny of other nations.

Q. PETER C. LUDZ, *The University of Munich; Graduate Faculty, The New School for Social Research*

I have some reservations about Professor Schwab's statements. In the instance of *Ostpolitik*, the Bonn government certainly exercised sovereign power. What we should do is discuss what is meant by sovereign power. I think that Professor Schwab has approached the question of power very narrowly.

A. GEORGE SCHWAB, *The City University of New York*

I agree that I have somewhat overstated the point. I should have qualified my assertion by drawing a distinction between the ability to make fundamental political decisions and incidental ones. No one will deny that Bonn, Paris, and London have room to maneuver politically and thus make incidental political decisions which may, in the long run, have fundamental repercussions.

HANS J. MORGENTHAU, *Graduate Faculty, The New School for Social Research*

In so far as people have a choice they have power; for

example, the choice to stay or not to stay in NATO, to join or not to join the common front of oil consuming nations. Because Germany, France, and Great Britain have choices they have power. The choices are, of course, more limited than they were a half century ago, but they exist.

Q. JOHN H. HERZ, *The City University of New York*

In your paper, Professor Schwab, you have said something about drawing lines somewhere. Where should these be drawn? Could these include those that have been established by *Ostpolitik*?

A. GEORGE SCHWAB, *The City University of New York*

Certainly not. I am particularly concerned about gray areas. Yugoslavia is one example. Perhaps even Rumania. I have nightmares about the Persian Gulf region.

Q. DANKWART A. RUSTOW, *The City University of New York*

Would you favor laying down exact geographic lines which we claim for us against the Russians?

A. GEORGE SCHWAB, *The City University of New York*

The Soviet Union has done so. Recently it has reasserted itself over Czechoslovakia and Hungary. It is in our interest to draw our own lines. I hope that one day we will not find ourselves in the predicament whereby others will decide for us where our lines should be.

HANS J. MORGENTHAU, *Graduate Faculty, The New School for Social Research*

On the question of lines in Europe, I have one basic disagreement with Professor Schlesinger. The presence of our military forces in West Germany has not only performed a symbolic function in assuring West Germany of our resolution to defend it, but it has also signaled to the Russians, if you cross the lines of demarcation of 1945, you will automatically be at war with the United States. The presence of American troops in Western Europe, particularly in West Germany, is of such political and military importance that I fully agree with the insistence of the Administration and the present majority in Congress on the necessity of maintaining our military posture in that part of the world.

Q. WERNER CAHNMAN, *Rutgers University*

Professor Rustow, you say what I have heard frequently said but without any documentation, namely, that it is not in the interest of the Soviet Union to have Israel militarily destroyed. Could you please explain your assertion.

A. DANKWART A. RUSTOW, *The City University of New York*

The reason I said it was not in the Soviet interest to see Israel destroyed is that Israel's presence has been the greatest single obstacle to Arab relations with the West and the major reason why some Arab countries have sought the support of the Soviet Union. This can be easily documented. The Khrushchev-Nasser arms deal of 1955 would not have come about without the presence of Israel. Nor might it have come about if the United States had not reneged on earlier arrangements with Egypt as regards the Aswan Dam.

Q. KEITH EUBANK, *The City University of New York*

Professor Rustow was talking about the fact that the United States had forced Israel to halt its victorious war about a year ago. I am very much interested in two questions: (1) was that related to detente? and (2) suppose the United States had not done that, what would have been the result?

A. DANKWART A. RUSTOW, *The City University of New York*

The first question is an easy question. I am not sure exactly what happened between Washington and Moscow almost exactly a year ago. Kissinger at one point promised us some publication of documents on which he simply reneged. On arriving in the Middle East he must have assumed that he had perhaps some Soviet agreement to stop the war jointly, as it were. When I said that we stopped an

Israeli victory or words to that effect I was speaking in extreme abbreviation, for which I apologize. Confronted by a two-front war, the Israelis had to throw all their resources on the Golan Heights first as a more immediate danger than the Sinai front. Once in control of the situation in the north and with the army fully mobilized, they were then beginnning to do pretty well in the Sinai. There they were well on the way to encircling one of the Egyptian armies, and in fact insisted on completing the operation after the official cease fire the first time around, and then came the American threat somewhere along the line that the United States would not give any ammunition and other supplies unless the Israelis complied with the cease fire. This is when Dayan made the statement I quoted. When the military balance was beginning to tip in Israel's favor, the Americans intervened to redress the balance.

What would have happened if the Israelis had encircled one Egyptian army or the two of them? I do not feel like Professor Morgenthau, who replied to the Tass correspondent from Moscow that he does not like to speculate about the future. I think it certainly would have made a difference and things would look a little better for Israel now.

GEORGE SCHWAB, *The City University of New York*

Permit me to make an observation on the question of the Middle East. I find Kissinger's policy disastrous. While amply supplying Israel with arms so that in the next round Israel should not employ tactical nuclear weapons (in this sense Israel has boxed the United States into a corner), Kissinger is at the same time narrowing Israel's maneuverability. I think it obvious that to pacify the Arabs, Kissinger, perhaps unintentionally, may succeed in totally Finlandizing Israel, thereby paving the way for its political demise. Once Israel has been Finlandized and dismembered, it stands to reason that the Arabs will have no further use for a Soviet presence and hence kick them out. Obviously, this would be a victory for the United States. As history is known to play tricks on us all, it is not inconceivable that, if the Soviet Union were faced with the possibility of expulsion from the region, its continued interests there on the one hand, and Israel's interest in political survival on the other hand, may then openly converge. The possibility that the Soviet Union would thus become an active champion of Israel's political existence cannot, therefore, be precluded—something Israel is sure to welcome. Should this ever occur, the United States will not only have failed in its endeavor to curtail drastically or expel completely the Soviet presence from this vital region, but it will also have succeeded in sacrificing its only stable natural political ally in the area, a liberal democracy.

Q. ROBERTO SOCAS, *Essex County College, N.J.*

My question is addressed to Professor Schlesinger. The problem of domestic political considerations does intrude heavily into the issue of detente. Senator Jackson does support emigration of Soviet Jews and greater humanity by the Soviets similar to the position Professor Schlesinger supports. One could wonder if Senator Jackson would be supportive of Soviet Jews if he did not feel that Jews constituted a sizeable voting bloc in the United States. One can perhaps become somewhat cynical of his motivation. However, can one not argue that it is not patriotic for Americans to support the flight of Soviet Jewry. Professor Schwab has argued that the Soviets benefit by being able to get rid of troublesome, unhappy dissidents. Looking back on the Cuban issue, perhaps one can argue that had the United States prohibited dissidents, unhappy Cubans from coming to the United States, Castro would have been overthrown years ago. Can one not argue, therefore, that our detente policy should not include a trade-off for humanitarian purposes.

A. ARTHUR M. SCHLESINGER, JR., *The City University of New York*

The situation in Cuba is distinct from the situation in the

Soviet Union. Two hundred fifty thousand refugees in Dade County, Florida, represent a much larger proportion of the Cuban population than the proportion of the Russian population represented by the very small number of Jews likely to leave the Soviet Union in the next decade. In many cases the Cuban refugees are more centrally located from the point of view of the power arrangements within Cuba. Apart from intellectual freedom, Jews want to leave the U.S.S.R. because of the legacy of racial repression. They have decided that they have no hope in Russia. It is very apparent that an intellectual like Solzhenitsyn was not in the least inclined to leave the Soviet Union. Expulsion was a severe punishment, directly devised for him, for, he thought, he could fight the system from within.

Q. STEPHANIE NEUMAN, *Graduate Faculty, The New School for Social Research*

Professor Schlesinger, I wonder if you would care to comment on what you think the function of foreign policy and diplomacy is and should be. Where does liberalization stop? Once historians and political scientists are given freedom of expression, how far, on the next round of trade negotiations, do we then pressure for a two-party system and a secret ballot? Secondly, why should the Soviet Union only be honored by our concern for intellectual freedom? Why not China, Yugoslavia, and a whole host of other countries?

A. ARTHUR M. SCHLESINGER, JR., *The City University of New York*

This is precisely why I was opposed to the Jackson amendment. On the other hand, speaking practically, and in this particular and very special situation, there is no question that Congressional consideration of the Jackson amendment has brought about some beneficial changes. I would hate to generalize from that to a notion that a function of diplomacy should be to induce internal changes in other countries. I cannot think of anything more likely to inflame the already considerable self-righteousness of the American government and the American people.*

Q. HERBERT STRAUSS, *The City College of New York*

Professor Schlesinger's assumption is that a liberalized society would of necessity be a more peaceful society. I would call this the Mazzini-Wilson illusion. But nineteenth century international politics and history throws serious doubts on this Wilsonian position. Do you believe that a liberalization of Soviet domestic life would really bring fundamental changes in Soviet foreign policy?

A. ARTHUR M. SCHLESINGER, JR., *The City University of New York*

I don't think that a more liberal society is necessarily a more peaceful society. I tried to guard myself against the Mazzini-Wilson fallacy by saying the difference was that, if liberal societies decide to go to war, at least the critics of the government can be overheard in their account of the government's intention.

KLAUS PRINGSHEIM, *McMaster University, Canada*

On the question of detente I am able to provide a sidelight. Recently there was a conference in Banff, Canada. It was a joint conference of the American-Slavic association, the Canadian-Slavic association, and the British-Slavic association. In the main conference area there was a table manned by some Ukrainian students who were asking people to sign up for some support of Valentyn Moroz, the Ukrainian historian. The Soviet Union sent a twelve-man delegation, and it interjected its views into the various panels at the meetings to no particular good effect, but at least to label most of the scholars present as bourgeois falsifiers, etc. The head of the delegation also protested to the head of the conference about the provocative nature of the presence of a table at which Valentyn Moroz was being championed. When this was heard by some of the Americans at the conference, they took it upon themselves at 2:30

*or, as the event showed, to set back Soviet-American trade relations

A.M. to transport that table to another building away from the main conference area. This, despite warnings that they should not do this, because the Ukrainian students might set fire to the building or do something else. I think this is at least partly illustrative of the length to which the United States State Department and other agencies are willing to go to promote detente. I would also like to comment on some definitions of detente that have occurred to me. It seems to me that the policy of detente is perhaps to keep on smiling no matter how uncomfortable you feel because the Russians are hitting you in the stomach, or possibly the policy of detente is one in which the United States gives everything to the Soviet Union that it could possibly need in terms of trade and aid. We sold the Russians millions of tons of grain and we then lent them the money to buy it, via the Chase Manhattan Bank. This is very nice indeed, and in return for all this largesse we received assurances from the Russians that they will not commit suicide by attacking us.

# NOTES ON CONTRIBUTORS

GIL CARL ALROY is a professor of political science at Hunter College and is also on the doctoral faculty at The City University Graduate School. A Princeton Ph.D., Professor ALRoy was also a member of Princeton's Center of International Studies. He is currently a member of the Executive Committee of The National Committee on American Foreign Policy; his publications include *The Kissinger Experience: American Policy in the Middle East.*

KEITH EUBANK is professor of history and chairman of the department at Queens College. A member of the doctoral faculty at The City University Graduate School, he received his Ph.D. from the University of Pennsylvania. Professor Eubank has also taught at Bloomfield College and North Texas State University. Among his publications is *The Origins of World War II.*

HENRY FRIEDLANDER is a professor of history in the Department of Jewish Studies at The City College of New York. A University of Pennsylvania Ph.D., Professor Friedlander has also taught at Louisiana State University in New Orleans, The University of Missouri in St. Louis, and McMaster University in Canada. He is on the Board of Directors of The National Committee on American Foreign Policy. His publications include *On the Holocaust.*

JOHN H. HERZ is a professor of political science at The City College of New York and a member of the doctoral faculty at The City University Graduate School. He received his Ph.D. from The University of Cologne. He has also taught at Columbia, The Fletcher School of Law and Diplomacy, The Graduate Faculty of The New School for Social Research, the University of Marburg, and The Free University of Berlin. His publications include *International Politics in the Atomic Age.*

GERTRUDE HIMMELFARB is a professor of history at Brooklyn College and Acting Executive Officer of the Doctoral Program in History at The City University Graduate School.

She holds the Ph.D. from the University of Chicago. Professor Himmelfarb is on the Board of Overseers of The Hoover Institution at Stanford University. Twice the recipient of Guggenheim fellowships, she is also a Fellow of The American Academy of Arts and Sciences and of The Royal Historical Society. Her most recent book is entitled *On Liberty and Liberalism.*

ERICH ISAAC is a professor of geography at The City College of New York and is also on the doctoral faculty at The City University Graduate School. He received the Ph.D. from Johns Hopkins, and has taught at Temple University. Professor Isaac has been a Ford Foundation Fellow in Africa and a Guggenheim Fellow, and is on the Board of Directors of The National Committee on American Foreign Policy. His publications include *The Geography of Domestication.*

PETER C. LUDZ is a professor of political science at The University of Munich, and for the academic year 1974-1975 Theodor Heuss Professor of Political Science at The New School for Social Research. Dr. Ludz received his Ph.D. from The Free University of Berlin, and he has also taught there, at Bielefeld, and at Columbia. A political adviser to the West German government since 1970, he has most recently published *Two Germanys in One World.*

HANS J. MORGENTHAU is University Professor of Political Science on the staff of The Graduate Faculty at The New School for Social Research. A University of Frankfurt J.U.D., Professor Morgenthau has taught at the universities of Geneva, Chicago, Columbia, Harvard, Yale, and The City College of New York and The City University Graduate School. A consultant to The Department of State, he is also Chairman of The National Committee on American Foreign Policy; among his books is *Politics Among Nations.*

DANKWART A. RUSTOW is Distinguished Professor of Political Science at Brooklyn College and The City University Graduate School. He received the Ph.D. degree from

Yale. Professor Rustow has also taught at Princeton, Columbia, Yale, Heidelberg, Harvard, and The London School of Economics. He is a former Vice President of the American Political Science Association and The Middle East Studies Association and a member of The Council on Foreign Relations. Among his publications is *Philosophers and Kings: Studies in Leadership*.

ARTHUR M. SCHLESINGER, JR. is Albert Schweitzer Professor of the Humanities at The City University Graduate School. Educated at Harvard and at Cambridge, Professor Schlesinger taught at Harvard before becoming Special Assistant to President Kennedy. Professor Schlesinger is a member of The Council on Foreign Relations. He has won the Pulitzer prize twice. His most recent book is *The Imperial Presidency*.

GEORGE SCHWAB is a professor of history at The City College of New York and a member of the doctoral faculty at The City University Graduate School. He received the Ph.D. from Columbia, and has also taught there. Professor Schwab is on the Board of Directors of The National Committee on American Foreign Policy. Among his publications is *The Challenge of the Exception: An Introduction to the Political Ideas of Carl Schmitt*.

# INDEX